www.carloswallace.com

LIFE IS NOT COMPLICATED—
YOU ARE

Turning Your Biggest Disappointments into Your Greatest Blessings

CARLOS WALLACE

LIFE IS NOT COMPLICATED— YOU ARE TURNING YOUR BIGGEST DISAPPOINTMENTS INTO YOUR GREATEST BLESSINGS

"Good Ol' Country Boy" painting
(Artist) Bill Sorrells, Jr., M.Ed.
www.billsorrellsjr.bigcartel.com/

Book cover designed by:
Deonne Moore
Skylimit Graphics

Photo on front cover:
Keena Wallace
KWallace Photography
www.kwallacephotography.net

iUniverse books may be ordered through booksellers or by contacting:

iUniverse
1663 Liberty Drive
Bloomington, IN 47403
www.iuniverse.com
1-800-Authors (1-800-288-4677)

ISBN: 978-1-4917-1564-2 (sc)
ISBN: 978-1-4917-1566-6 (hc)
ISBN: 978-1-4917-1565-9 (e)

Library of Congress Control Number: 2013921653

Print information available on the last page.

iUniverse rev. date: 02/24/2015

CONTENTS

My life must speak for me, when I can no longer speak for myself.

What others think about you should not frame your reality. Your past experiences should not deter you. The earlier you tap into this understanding, the sooner you begin living an uninhibited life. A life of purpose.

When you approach your past with an open mind, soaking up lessons like a sponge, you will no longer use it as an excuse to fail because it will become a reason to succeed. Your building blocks. Your foundation.

A diverse array of philosophers, poets, authors, spiritual shepherds and political leaders who mastered individual forms of expression yet they shared a common school of thought: each believed and informed at some point in their influential lives that experience is one of life's greatest teachers. I agree wholeheartedly and add, that while experience is a cogent pedagogue, adversity is its closest ally: the obstinate life coach.

V: FEARLESS

To know who you are is a source of great power. You are shielded from the debilitating effects of insecurity and doubt. You walk more proudly, stand taller, make better decisions, take control of your destiny.

VI: DISAPPOINTMENT

You can either let it consume you, until you become bitter and resentful. Or, you can accept what has happened, learn from it and move on. It really is that simple. What we tend to do is over analyze. We replay the circumstances over and over again, trying to extrapolate "Why me", "why now", "what if"? And while answers to these questions may bring you some peace of mind, it will not change the circumstances that disappointed you to begin with.

VII: DELIVERANCE

The big risk you take with deep reflection is you may not like the answers that rise to the surface. Still it's better to walk in clarity than it is to stumble aimlessly in darkness.

VIII: VALIDATION

While the unfavorable judgments of a few should not disappoint you, the flattery of many (while fantastic) should not delight you. In other words opinions, good or bad, should not influence your state of mind. Remember, the more you have to proclaim how great, smart, talented and desirable "people" say you are, the less you truly believe it. Braggers project to quiet their insecurity. Humility is a restrained expression of your finest qualities. Humble confidence lets your best speak for itself. This self-assuredness can only come if your inner-voice is the loudest.

IX: FREEDOM 99

X: LEGACY 109

XI: PHOENIX 119

XII: SUCCESS 131

XIII: FORWARD 143

FOREWORD

Carlos Wallace writes a compelling story about his life and the evolutionary influence those closest to him had on the development of his character and explores these relationships in a way that holds our attention and offers advice without lecturing us.

This book opens with an unexpected revelation and continues with a discussion of concepts which make us who we are as human beings. Greatest among these is the love for one another as evidenced in the warmth bestowed upon him by his mother and father and other relatives and how that love empowered him to rise to the challenges he faced growing up. Evidence of the "Golden Rule" is found throughout his expressive writing.

The chapters of a *Life Is Not Complicated, You Are* demonstrate great critical thinking and offer helpful insight into constructs that affect us all as we grow from youth through adulthood. These insights are consistent with the writings of John Bowlby and his Theory of Attachment and changes over the human lifespan. In fact, it should cause those of us who have already reached chronological maturity to reflect on having a greater understanding of ourselves and our world.

Carlos does not tell us how we should think or feel, but his writing leads us to a greater understanding of the guiding principles he has come to embrace and which have served him well thus far. Beginning with his "Purpose" and "Foundation", this life story continues with so many of the values we wish to recognize in ourselves, our children, our friends and our extended families.

Among the keywords noted, I was so glad to find terms such as "wisdom, role modeling, and humility, self- healing, and dealing with adversity and fear and self-doubt" addressed. Perhaps even more importantly, readers will enjoy his observations on personal freedom, faith, hope, responsibility, acceptance and self-love, forgiveness, commitment and loyalty.

Carlos Wallace understands that genuine reflection on our upbringing, good or bad, will allow us to make better choices in our life, or at least, to minimize the mistakes we have all made from time to time. He notes that the legacy we will leave to those who survive us is entirely within our control and that we should never waste the opportunity to ensure that this legacy is one we can be as proud of in life, as it will be in death.

John A. Nadalin, Ph.D.
Adjunct Professor
Business Psychology
Franklin University

DEDICATION:

For my loving mother, Alice Hunt Wallace, my friend and my inspiration. In spirit she forever guides me. Momma was strong, passionate, stubborn and proud. An educator and wife, she was both fearless and vulnerable and unashamed of either. My mother demanded the best, especially of me and I dedicate my life to exceeding her highest expectations.

For my children, my Legacy. Whether my blood courses through your veins, we are bound by a mutual love, or you have lovingly adopted me as Dad, know that I cherish you and thank God everyday for bringing you into my life. I love you all. If I am half the father to you guys as mine was to me, I will have fulfilled my greatest Purpose.

"Country Boy 2"
Orig. Drawing
Charcoal/Watercolor
by Bill Sorrells
for Carlos Wallace

INTRO: "GOOD OL' COUNTRY BOY FROM EAST TEXAS"

The *"Good Ol' Country Boy"* image is the quintessential illustration of my life's story.

I did not grow up privileged or with any haughty pre-conceived notions about our family's standing in our community, despite the fact my mother was a noted educator and my grandfather a highly regarded Justice. We did not worship the dollar, we worshipped God. The term "family" extended well beyond the limits of DNA placing the task of raising children in the hands of mother, father, grandparent and neighbor. We were all kinfolk. Defying authority was a potentially unforgivable affront. Respect, loyalty, love and our faith were requisites throughout the small town. Life was simple then because these principles were consistent, accepted ideologies that were understood by most. These inherent lessons provided me with the wherewithal to tackle challenges.

I am extremely proud of my humble beginnings. I make it my mission to live up to and hopefully exceed the expectations of every single person who sacrificed blood, sweat and tears to set me on the right path. These basic, albeit critical, small country town principles enriched my life in ways affluence or prominent social standing could not. Fundamental, unpretentious lessons that set the stage for how I would comport myself every day in an overly complicated world. Today the duality of my character is obvious: beneath the surface of a strong willed, honorable, hard working family man and altruist beats the simple heart of a *Good Ol' Country Boy* from East Texas.

GENESIS

For as far back as I can remember, I was taught there is zero room for excuses. This means I have a long, busy, challenging road ahead. But as the old adage goes, life is a journey, not a destination. I'm in it for the long haul, and looking forward to every second.

I

The intensity of the game in progress inside the segregated gymnasium filled the air with so much heat that if you looked close enough you could see the steam rise from the highly polished hard wood floors. The gym had a pulse. And for the last hour the steady, rhythmic beat came from one source, and her vigorous efforts escalated with every shot. The star basketball player had been running her opponents into a dizzied state of confusion this last quarter. Her teammates laid the entire weight of this game squarely on her shoulders, a charge that only made her play harder, despite the searing pain ripping through her abdomen. Her body had been sending her alarming signals all night, but there was no way she was going to let something as simple as a cramp break her concentration. With every pivot, every foul, every three-point play-and there were quite a few-the pressure radiated through her back, causing her muscles to seize and relax in split second intervals. Spectators watched in disbelief as the countdown to the buzzer seemed to hang in the air as long as the last incredible shot weaving its way nimbly through the net. 20 points. And then, the pain in her stomach exploded as wildly as the cheering students now reacting with crazed frenzy in the bleachers. Whatever it was that wanted her attention more than this critical game challenged her focus much more than the defense that hovered like a menacing guard; sweaty, aggressive sentinels fighting to put an end to the embarrassing athleticism that threatened to rip victory from the team favored to win this game. 24 points.

She had grown accustomed to pushing through pain. Growing up in the discriminatory throes of the civil rights movement certainly prepared her for obstacles. Her biggest defense played out on the streets, in her school and right outside the safety of her home every day. She would have succumbed to the pressure long ago were it not for a strong father who protected his home and children by arming them with confidence, spiritual fortitude and rapier intellect, and her devoted mother. Instead, she endured the strain. She allowed it to feed her strength, satiate her resolute spirit and transform her into an unstoppable force to be reckoned with.

One could argue she had become immune to all hardship, for how else could she manage to play through what was slowly becoming a full-throttle assault on her game-worn body. Call it adrenaline, will power, divine intervention-or just plain stubborn resilience-but as the clock ticked off its final ten seconds, she managed one final burst of power that seemed to come from the depths of her womb. What had nearly crippled her with pain somehow coursed through her very being, awakening every cell in a way that even shocked her. As her heart pounded uncontrollably, she tapped into this yet unknown source of power, spun with tamed precision, eluded her flustered defense to drive a hard line down the center of the court, and with a subtle pause and an almost imperceptible aching smile, launched the winning shot.

And then, utter madness ensued. The crowd flooded the court waving banners and filling the air with gut bending cheers. There was of course the chorus of boos that wafted through the celebration, a sharp reminder that they (she) were not welcome. It was also the sound that snapped her out of her moment glory and confirmed that she had not imagined the grinding pain that now buckled her knees. The room spun out of control, and the sounds around her merged into a piercing cacophony of high-pitched screams and woeful moans. Her moans.

Hours later, she lay in the hospital, her head still pulsating from her sudden fall to the hardwood. She remembered, in flashes, the doctors asking her to breathe, and then push. Relax, then push. Take a deep breath and then one more big push. And moments later, she heard it: the unmistakable, persistent wail that would soon explain the source of her cutting pain, and the origin of the uninhibited strength that led her to victory and brought her the deepest joy. As the doctor placed her newborn son gently into her arms she knew his ceremonious, unrelenting entry into the world was a prologue; together they had just overcome one of the most excruciating and challenging experiences in their lives. This reality would, for 27 years, define the breadth and depth of their unbreakable bond. It would also shape the intriguing life of a man who learned to expect the unexpected, make the most of every circumstance and most importantly, that you cannot just live life; you must share insights acquired from the life you have lived.

I'm Carlos Wallace. This true story of my first day of life, my *genesis*, inspires me. From the beginning, my journey has not been easy, but it has been determined. The path I travelled was littered with personal landmines. It was also paved with victories. Fortunately, I was never alone on my journey and for that I am eternally grateful.

Understand, no one can make it through life without the help and kindness of others. Nor should they have to. You are not on a solitary trek into the unknown. Your path is pre-determined by God, and his angels are strategically placed along the way. I found mine. Let's find yours. Welcome to my world. Take what you need.

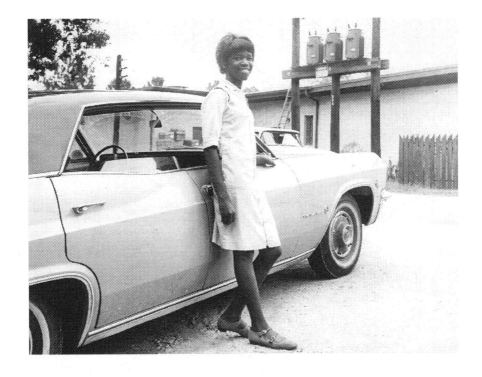

PURPOSE

Few things are more liberating than knowing who you are, what you want, and what you'll do to get there. Don't let anyone blur that focus with naysaying and unsolicited advice. When you succeed, you'll be surprised how the chorus changes from "You're foolish to try" to "I knew you could! Now, can you help me out?" Decide your own future and no one can lay claim to your success!

II

I have lived my life thus far with few regrets. Adopting this mindset has not been easy, but I assure you it is possible and quite necessary if you want peace of mind. You will learn though, that this is a powerful state of being you will not reach overnight. It is a process, which begins with your willingness to release your hold on the past and believe that everything in life happens for a reason. Sure, this requires a leap of faith that many are not prepared -or inclined- to take for any number of reasons. Perhaps you do not identify with a so-called higher power. Perhaps you are pragmatic and unable to embrace beliefs you cannot verify. Or maybe you are not confident enough to recognize that you are not defined by your past or the people in it. Buddha teaches "Do not dwell in the past, do not dream of the future; concentrate the mind on the present moment." We spend so much time worried about what *if* that we lose sight of and fail to engage the more progressive attitude of what *is*. When we obsess about what if, it causes us to question who we are today, in the present. We harbor some unresolved notion that, had circumstances been different, we would be different; we would somehow, be better. And since there is nothing you can do to change the past you hang awkwardly in this insecure limbo of self-doubt. However, if you dissociate yourself from experiences that cannot be altered and focus on circumstances you can control, you will realize that you are very powerful. As arbiter of your life you can choose how you feel, how you react and what you want to achieve. *You* give your life direction and meaning. You give your life, purpose.

There is considerable freedom attached to knowing and accepting who you are. Fortunately, I never really had to struggle with my identity. My mother loved me from the moment I was conceived.

I know this because she told me, often. Not that she needed to reassure me, although it was wonderful to hear. From the time I could reasonably understand what it meant to be loved, her affection encouraged and empowered me. More importantly, she taught me to love myself. I became comfortable in my own skin. It is a trait I relish and for good reason. It arms me with exactly what I need to overcome the most daunting challenges in order to break from that what if mentality and engage what is.

I believe the power of embracing who you are is disturbingly underrated and that failing to do so is dangerously debilitating. Life is much less complicated when you no longer focus on how the criticism, opinions and self-loathing of others affect you. For instance, I take extreme pride in my appearance. Save a brief lapse in confidence about the age of eight (which I will expound on in a later chapter) I always have, even though I grew up in an age when, in my community, it was not popular to be dark skinned. Fairer skinned young men and women were more inclined to be asked out on dates, voted Homecoming King and Queen or cast for prime roles in school plays. I cycled through this period relatively unfazed. Now, by today's standards -and with the understanding that beauty is in the eye of the beholder -some may consider me attractive. This is partly because I meticulously maintain my appearance. Not to mention, these days we are more inclined to see darker skinned actors, actresses, models and even sports figures being recognized as handsome or beautiful. However, as a child and then a teenager growing up in the 1970s I was teased, overlooked and shunned because, in the words of some of my peers, I was "so black". The cruelty was not limited to bullies my age. Adults also wielded merciless pre-conceptions. I realize now that most of them were probably battling their own self-loathing. Still, if it weren't for my mother, who raised me to be a proud person, I would have been felled by the belittling perceptions of others. Eventually, my self-assurance became an extension of my ebony complexion. I understood that I was smart, intuitive, resourceful, reliable and full of integrity. I was all that wrapped in a dark, bold package. I wore my confidence like body armor. Still do.

I modeled my personality, mind-set and my essence after the blueprint of genuine acceptance that my loving mother helped draft. Truth is, the public will either love you, hate you or will be indifferent, plain and simple. You determine if they *respect* you. That is what matters. The rest is superficial. What others think about you should not frame your reality. Your experiences should not deter you. The earlier you tap into this understanding, the sooner you will begin living an uninhibited life. You will live a life of purpose. Confidence is a powerful incentive. It is also deliriously intoxicating. I never had to search far for the origin of this natural high because it was right in my backyard, literally.

My family history is rich with inspiration. Most generations can respectfully claim a prominent success story. My grandfather, the Honorable Judge O'Neal Hunt, the first African American justice to hold the position in Palestine, Texas is mine. Not a single day passes when I am not reminded of a lesson he taught me. And believe me, he was an extremely generous teacher. I remember one instance in particular.

If you browse through my pictures or happen to see me with a group of close friends and family, you will find I am always smiling and joking around. I smile and laugh as much as possible because it is healing. And because there was a period in my life when I did not smile much, if at all. In fact, I was one angry young man. I was particularly angry at what I believed the America I was raised in represented, especially racial inequality. I also felt that my level of intelligence betrayed me by opening my eyes to the aforementioned reality while those around me ignored the rampant injustice. As far as I was concerned, we had a ways to go with regard to the fragile state of race relations in America. These feelings were heightened upon my return from Desert Storm.

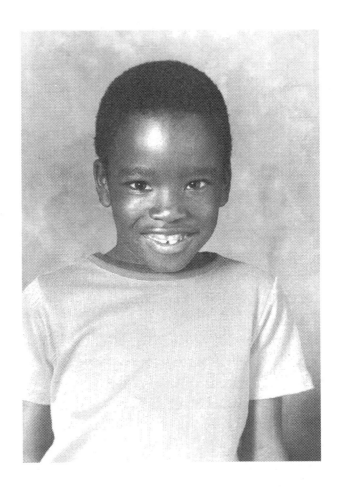

Carlos Wallace is promoted to petty officer third class

As a result of the Navy- wide advancement exam administered in March, Carlos Wallace advanced to Petty Officer Third Class.

Wallace works in the field of radio communications. His job consists of radio satellite and fleet secure voice communications. Along with communications, he also works with a great deal of classified material which requires a top secret security clearance.

While onboard the U.S.S. Dubuque (LPD-8), Wallace has shown outstanding leadership skills in his rate. At the same time he has become qualified in special shipboard personal qualification stations such as damage control, advance damage control, 3M maintenance, and sound powered phone talker. Along with those special qualifications, he has participated in special exercises, such as Operation Desert Shield/Storm, Valiant Usher in the Philippine Sea, and Team Spirit '91 in Pusan Korea.

In such a concise tour on board the U.S.S. Dubuque, Wallace has received such awards as: The National Defense Medal, Southwest Asian Sea Medal, Sea

CARLOS WALLACE

Service Ribbon, and two Letters of Appreciation for outstanding performance.

Wallace is the son of Mr. and Mrs. Aaron Wallace of Jacksonville. The grandson of Mrs. Corsie Lee Wallace of Jacksonville and Judge and Mrs. O'Neal Hunt of Palestine.

I do not look back on those years frequently. Once you have shed a layer of character that is so unflattering and burdensome, you leave it where it falls and pray it decomposes and disappears forever. When the sentiment was at its tipping point and I was about to lose myself in a miserable abyss of my own making, Granddaddy reached down and pulled me back from the brink, teaching me things about life and myself that I carry in my heart to this day.

My grandfather and I talked often. He was one of few people who could look into my eyes and know exactly what I was feeling. When Granddaddy addressed me it was always for a good reason. He was never one to allow emotion to cloud his judgment or to speak just for the sake of hearing his own voice. One evening, during one of my many visits, and when I was at my most discontent, I asked him how he, a jurist who lived through the injustice and degradation of the civil rights movement; who was made to feel like he was less than a man, less than a human being; who was judged, tried and socially convicted based solely on the color of his skin, was able to apportion unbiased justice to people who *looked like* the ones who made his life a living hell. I distinctly remember the situation that made me ask that pointed question.

Granddaddy was approached by a young man who found himself on the wrong side of a minor infraction that could have led to major complications in the future. My grandfather went out of his way to ensure that the man received a shot at a second chance, an opportunity some may argue he did not deserve. Suffice it to say, the guy was thrilled. And while the unexpected reprieve was a relief, I think the lesson in compassion my grandfather imparted would help him walk the straight and narrow from that point. I was impressed of course, but stumped. Granddaddy went above and beyond for a white man who by all accounts should have suffered the repercussions of his actions. And I wondered how he could act so selflessly in light of his experiences with the race that persecuted him. When I posed the question, he did not respond angrily or berate me for what could only be described as my haughty ignorance. He looked right at me and said, "Baby, it is not for me to judge him. He is judged by the law. A law I vowed to practice and respect as a Judge and an honorable man. If the law fails, a greater judgment awaits at the end of that man's life. Either way, it is out of my hands". I was speechless. And impressed.

I will not lie and say that his words changed my heart immediately. But over the years as I witnessed my grandfather practice what he preached and lead by example every moment of his life, I began to understand that I cannot allow bitterness and hate to dictate my decisions. I cannot treat others with disdain for acts they did not personally commit. Ultimately, I should not punish one man for another man's sins. This is, by far, one of the greatest, most profound lessons Granddaddy imparted. Dare I say, it saved my life. I shed my anger, slowly. And I worked hard every day to find reasons to appreciate my life and forgive those who I felt wronged me. Once I did that, I found (and kept) my smile.

To me, O'Neal Hunt was bigger than life, the true definition of a hero. Just saying his name, recalling his spirit, awakens a sense of awe inside me that burns white hot. Granddaddy was a man of God, a loyal husband and a devoted family man who possessed a wisdom that traced the narrow, perilous passages of a difficult, albeit fulfilling life. His actions never strayed from his philosophy. He could command attention without ever raising his voice; his mere presence spoke volumes. He earned respect by virtue of his disciplined work ethic, his integrity and his constant hunger for knowledge and enlightenment. Granddaddy stood as tall and unmovable as a mighty oak, yet possessed a sense of compassion that ran as fluidly and serenely as a crystal clear stream; indeed, his sense of clarity was one of the greatest gifts he left me.

Today, I want you to ask yourself, if you had to choose one person who inspires you, who would that person be? Who is your O'Neal Hunt? That person who, no matter what, fuels your desire to just be better, whether it is because they accomplished something great or because they choose to lead a righteous life? It could be a philanthropist or the mom next door who makes sure her children are always well behaved, clean, educated. Perhaps it is a pastor, rabbi or imam. My point is, identify someone in your daily life who inspires you. They are role models who prove you can accomplish anything you set your mind to despite your past. These people have a very valuable gift. Gifts much like my grandfather and my mom gave to me, including clarity and confidence. These are keys that unlocked my mind, freed me from doubt and insecurity and fueled my intense desire to embrace the present.

These are the gift of Purpose.

FOUNDATION

No one makes it to the "top" by themselves. Each step you take is guided by at least one person's blood, sweat and tears. If you don't appreciate those who stand behind you as you rise, don't expect them to catch you if you fall. The ladder of success is steadiest when someone's there to support it.

III

I am proud to say that no matter where I am in life, in my heart I am and will always be just a regular ol' boy from East Texas. The city of Jacksonville, where I was born and raised, will always hold a special place in my heart. Some people choose to forget where they came from and I understand. People typically take good memories for granted. They also want to forget bad memories. However, the latter creates a complex paradox. Suppressing memory (which by definition is the mental capacity to retain facts, events or impressions) is contrary to normal cognitive function. You are fighting the power of the mind to remember things. This repression is a defense mechanism. It's also a temporary fix. Dr. Susan Kraus Whitbourne, author of the *Essential Guide to Defense Mechanisms* says, "Repression, like denial, can be temporarily beneficial, particularly if you've forgotten something bad that happened to you, but as with denial, if you don't come to grips with the experience it may come back to haunt you".[1] Your foundation is important. Discounting its relevance is a sure way to lose your way later in life. Every part of one's upbringing plays a substantial role in the person you are. Exploring the deep recesses of your heritage can be enlightening. In some cases, it can save your life. According to the Centers for Disease Control, family members share their genes as well as their environment, lifestyles and habits. Your hair and eye color, athletic ability and quirky behavior are inherited traits. Risks for diseases such as asthma, diabetes, cancer, and heart disease also run in families. One thing is for sure; you will never understand anything you ignore. This includes your heritage.

You may be saying, "Well, earlier you said we should let go of the past in order to move on." Please, do not misunderstand. I believe wholeheartedly that you should not let your past hold you back. However, you still need to learn from your experiences and be aware of your history. Find out the who, what, where, and how that led you to this point in your life so you can fully understand and embrace who you are. When you approach your past with an open mind, soaking up lessons like a sponge, you will no longer use it as an excuse to fail because it will become a reason to succeed. It will become your foundation.

I often hear friends and acquaintances say, "I don't know why I am unhappy" or, "I don't know why I am the way I am". Well, in order to have an understanding of exactly who you are, you need to know your lineage. Alex Haley wrote, "In every conceivable manner, the family is link to our past, bridge to our future."[2] I reflect on my past often. Some of it is painful. Still, most recollections are joyous. However there is never a meaningless memory.

---

[1]   Dr. Susan Kraus Whitbourne, "Essential Guide to Defense Mechanisms," *Psychology Today*, Oct. 2011,

[2]   Alex Haley, *Roots: The Saga of an American Family* (USA: Doubleday, 1976),

I want to know everything about my past. My ancestors lift me up. Their struggle, their triumphs and their fears are visceral. I am a product of working men and women: preachers, business professionals, labor leaders and homemakers. The biggest blessing was, and still is, the family unit and the nucleus of my family unit were my mother and my grandfather. When they passed on, everything and everyone slowly began to dissipate. Still, the foundation remained. I can return to East Texas and still find a vestige of the life I once had and appreciated. Elders that can stop me in my tracks with one look. Cousins who know what it was like to laugh and enjoy lazy summer days. Friends that reminisce about school days and mischievous acts. These moments are my anchor. They keep me grounded.

So many of us lack a basis, a beginning, a reason for why we are here. When you do not have someone to admire or emulate, finding your way is difficult. It fills you with loneliness. There is a void that cannot be filled with material possessions. We need to find our anchors and embrace our origins. If it hurts, begin to heal. If it inspires, soak it in. If it brings you happiness, carry it with you every day. You will not gain a thing by turning your back on history. It establishes your narrative. Just because you choose not to remember your history, does not mean it did not happen.

I have met a lot people in my life. Those closest to me have shared stories that broke my heart, including tales of domestic violence, molestation and mental and emotional abuse; memories of absentee fathers and the subsequent *daddy issues*, bi-polar mothers and aunts who never seemed happy; and the *bad uncle* who stole their innocence. Their recollections helped me understand them and strengthened our bonds. What's more, those who took the time to shake the family tree hoping critical answers would fall to earth, eventually gained a better understanding of self. That knowledge, that foundation, fosters growth. Positive growth.

I realize a lot of what I write may be easier said than done. Many of you may be dealing with more than you think you can manage on your own. Whether you call your burden issues, baggage, demons or problems, one thing is for sure; the burden weighs you down and wears you out. While I will never tell anyone what I believe is wrong with him or her since only a trained medical specialist should ever diagnose mental or physical ailments, I can say from experience that when I stopped thinking I had to deal with everything by myself and tapped into my well of support, the load got so much lighter. My struggles did not disappear nor did my concerns or fears evaporate into thin air. But the pressure, the stress, was mercifully alleviated. And it wasn't just about the good friends and family I surround myself with. It was about reaching way back and asking "What would my Momma do?" or "What would Granddaddy say?" It is a spiritual resource, a deep-seated salve; a comforting reserve that comes from my heart. We all have that personal remedy stored somewhere within us. Choose to accept it. It is nurtured by your memories, your past experiences. Blocking it out does you more harm than good.

Furthermore, do not think too much about the possibility that the people who hurt you will somehow *get it back* one day. Not because you are so forgiving or kind hearted, but because it is more fulfilling to be thankful for the experiences and people that challenged you. Those trials likely taught you so much about yourself, your potential and your spirituality. They help you appreciate the good things more. Strengthen you in ways you never imagined! Why would you ever hope that people who helped enlighten you suffer? Learn to Bless and Release! Besides, we should be so pre-occupied with living a better, more promising life that contemplating the fate of those who caused us pain is not even an option.

I have lived my life with unwavering commitment to everything I hold dear: my career, my family, my values and my God. I can look in the mirror and be proud of the image looking back at me. A life well lived, is truly a blessing. I lost both my parents before I reached the age of 40. My grandparents had long since left my life. Financial and personal disappointment could have leveled me had it not been for my ability to tackle these tragedies head on realistically. Instead of folding into myself and dwelling in discontent and sorrow, I chose to use my experiences to become stronger. I pushed myself to move forward and clear these emotional hurdles, not because I am any more mentally and spiritually balanced or capable than any one else, but because I just decided long ago it is better to use experiences to build me up, not break me down. I took charge of my life before something or someone took control and set me on a divergent path. We all have the ability to exercise the same drive. This propulsion to rise above challenges is fueled from within and is sometimes stoked by hard lessons.

The year 1982 marked a major turning point in my life. While other kids my age were struggling with puberty, preparing for Junior High, sharpening their skills on video games like Donkey Kong, Pac Man and Centipede, I was entering the workforce. That year I became an official tax-paying American. I was 11-years old. I did not know it back then, but my job as a paperboy in my small town of Jacksonville would teach me some of the greatest lessons I would learn about my family and myself.

The timing of my unceremonious but welcome introduction to employment was predicated by necessity. I had always recognized the value of responsibility, simply because it was instilled in me very early on. The time was ripe. It was then that this East Texas boy developed material cravings that were contrary to his humble origins. Consequently, I was forced to accept a sobering reality: my childhood wants far overshadowed my parents' tolerance for the contemporary trappings of the day. Their philosophy was ironclad. They provide everything I need to survive and flourish. Their hard-working dollars were reserved for maintaining the household and securing the well-being of everyone within its walls. I was fed, clothed, educated and loved. If I wanted the latest pair of hot sneakers, I would have to earn the money to buy them and in doing so, I could not let my grades suffer, ever. This was par for the course in the Wallace household. As the oldest of five children, I was not only encouraged to set an example, I was expected to. I always complied, but not without some resentment. However, I was also taught children should be seen and not heard so I kept my frustration close to the vest.

So, I began working every weeknight and immediately after school. And bright and early on Sunday when I mounted my bike at 3 a.m. to make my deliveries. Also on Sundays, with my Mom watching vigilantly from our car, I would collect my fees, bring the money to Jacksonville Daily Progress and wait eagerly as the editor calculated my earnings. And as I calculated how much I would spend my hard-earned paycheck, I was informed that my newfound fiscal freedom came with a catch. I had to pay our family's cable bill. Every month. Suffice it to say, I never questioned the reasoning behind this request and I also never missed a payment. Nor did I ever miss a day of work in the five years I was employed by the newspaper. The experience laid the groundwork for my work ethic and financial responsibility. And while I did not understand it at that time, it taught me discipline.

Many years after my first job was a distant memory, and a few weeks following my return from Operation Desert Storm, I visited with my Mom. Somehow we began to reminisce about the years she made her 11-year old son pay for the family's cable bill. Her reflections on that period surprised me. Her smile as she told the story, while warm, belied a deep pain. However, what nearly unsettled me completely was the seriousness in her voice. She did not apologize for asking me to pay that bill, nor did I expect her to. Yet there was something in her tone, in her eyes that almost asked for my forgiveness. She explained softly that around the time I began working, my Dad became a victim of the massive lay-offs in the railroad industry. The industry struggled amid the deep economic recession that some believe was spurred by "Reagonomics", which refers to the economic policies promoted by President Ronald Reagan during the 1980s. What began as a lesson in accountability and discipline helped ease the dire financial needs of my family. While I viewed the contribution as a burden, I was actually helping my Mom and Dad. My parents were struggling to make ends meet and here I was, all of 11 years old- and until I was 16- unwittingly helping support my family. I never knew. None of us did. As my Mom put it, "It was not for you kids to know. Our job as parents was to take care of you, and we did. How we did was only for us to know. Children should not have to bear the weight of adult struggles".

I realized then, as I had so many times before, that nothing my parents did was arbitrary. Their actions always served as a well I could draw from whenever I was at a crossroads. Their struggles were never in vain. Their triumphs were a constant source of inspiration. I sincerely believe, thanks in part to these aspects of my foundation, that everything happens for a reason and we must do anything in our power, using the resources we have at our disposal, to survive. Contrary to what some may think, this straightforward approach to life is not callous, just practical. It is also less complicated.

When all is said and done, no one will work harder to improve your life than you. Not a single person besides you has your best interests at heart. At least that is the way it should be. You are the only person who knows what you need, what you have been through and where you want to be without any doubts. And if you do not know, you must not allow others, especially those who know little or nothing about you, to feed you answers. Sometimes, the answers you seek are buried in your legacy. Research your story, discover your history and understand where you have been in order to be confidant about where you are headed.

I love what Jacksonville taught me, and where it lead me. The good, the bad and the indifferent all helped shaped me. I may not live there anymore but it lives inside me. It is and will always be, my Foundation.

ADVERSITY

How can it be that you, an adult, cannot succeed in life because someone won't let you? Whether it is your boss, a family member or someone you are in a relationship with, no one can prevent you from accomplishing great things but you. The same power you give to people that you claim hold you back use to knock them out of your way!

IV

Albert Einstein, Mark Twain, Julius Caesar, Gandhi, Dr. Martin Luther King, Eleanor Roosevelt, John Keats, Confucius. These notable men and women, in my humble opinion, are some of the most respected and brilliant minds in history. I consider them a diverse group of philosophers, poets, authors, spiritual shepherds and political leaders who mastered their individual forms of expression while sharing what I find to be a common school of thought; that *experience* is one of life's greatest teachers. And while experience is a cogent pedagogue, I maintain that *adversity* is its closest ally, the obstinate life coach.

How one deals with difficult circumstances speaks to their character and is arguably a reliable gauge of their spirit. While many of us rarely know how we will respond to life's trials one thing is certain: most of us can choose whether to be leveled by misfortune or rise to the challenge. This concept of inherent strength is found throughout this book. I firmly believe once you adopt the attitude that you completely control how you cope with and how you manage life's tumultuous ebb and flow, you will have one of the key components to achieving peace of mind. You will face each day armed with the confidence that you can (and will) conquer misfortune.

Oftentimes, men and women underestimate how resilient they are. I spoke with many people while writing this chapter who admitted they have no idea how tough they are because they have not faced suffering that tested their resolve. They have not lost a loved one, a job, or dealt with a serious illness. I believe you won't know how tough you are until you are jolted by a situation that tests your mettle.

Ernest Hemingway wrote, "The world breaks everyone, and afterward, some are strong at the broken places".[3] My mother personified that quote. She seemed to lead a nondescript life. However, beneath the surface, the depth of her struggle was anything but ordinary. If you spent an hour with Alice Wallace, you understood that everyone has a story, a past. Experiences and memories coursing through their consciousness, which create the intricate watermarks of that person's character. Some of these anecdotes will never be revealed. Fortunately, my family shared generous details of their rich -and sometimes painful- history with me. They recounted stories so vivid, my mind would race with the harsh images as my mother and grandfather painted a picture of their legacy, especially what it was like to live during the civil rights era. I absorbed each word, each emotion, each expository moment like a sponge.

I recall one story that is a personal reminder no challenge is insurmountable. As a star basketball player -and well before the onset of Genesis- my mother and her college team travelled throughout the South to compete. It was customary after some of

---

[3]   Ernest Hemingway, "A Farewell To Arms", (New York: Scribner, 1929),

these games for the bus, full of tired and hungry players, coaches and chaperones to find a diner along the route home. Keep in mind, this was the segregated South during a time people of color were commonly confronted with the stinging, unapologetic pall of discrimination. One evening, after her entire team and all the coaches entered a local establishment, one of the coaches approached my mother. She explained, as gingerly as possible to a young woman who had given everything in her power to help win another game for her predominantly white team, that they were in a "whites only" restaurant and she had to eat her meal on the bus, alone. True to form, my mother did not argue. She told me that she barely showed any emotion. She took her dinner and walked back to the bus, head held high. If she did shed a tear, the diner's proprietor, her coaches and teammates never knew. On the contrary, she mustered all the stoicism possible to ensure they did not sense her humiliation.

Suffice it to say, the thought of my mother sitting on that bus, robbed of her dignity after a heated and exhausting game, infuriated me. She summarily dismissed my anger because, as she explained, I missed the essence of the story. Of course she was hurt. How could such indignation not defile one's every sensibility? Her point was, it was not about the slight. It was not about her bruised pride. Those feelings were incidental. When all was said and done, she just did what she had to do. She faced her reality. She didn't carry on, act out or pout. She didn't disrespect her coach, curse her teammates or get discouraged or resentful. It would have done her no good and probably would have made a bad situation even worse. Most importantly, she did not give up. The experience did not break her. Instead, it motivated her. From that day forward, my mother played every game with the heart of a warrior and graduated an All-American athlete.

I know my mom did not envision a similar experience for any of her children. An unfortunate event that occurred years later shattered that expectation.

Our family, in my opinion, was fairly stable. I was blessed with parents who loved me and my siblings and provided for our family. My grandparents were the love of my life and the most sincere example of what a family's core should resemble. As the oldest in my family, my brothers and sisters looked up to me, and I was careful to set a good example, be a leader. When I was nine years old, I learned that outside our home life was not as picturesque, and I needed a thick skin in order to wear the demanding title of leader.

When my peers think back to the fourth grade, I suspect that their memories are filled with chalkboards, textbooks, and class trips. Pop quizzes and math assignments that took all night to complete are perhaps the most traumatic incidents of that pre-pubescent period. And while I encountered all of the above "inconveniences" to a certain degree, I still worked hard to earn the respect of my peers and the recognition of my teachers. That day finally arrived, when I was voted President of Junior Historians. I was always a good student and a popular member of our class. However, this was literally the first time my peers unanimously acknowledged me as a leader. I beamed with pride and savored every moment of my newly earned position. My mom was beside herself with excitement, accepting her share of the credit for this grand achievement. She did gloat quite a bit, as I recall. The local newspaper agreed to photograph the new officers and my mom made sure I was dressed to impress that day. The crease in my slacks was rapier sharp. My hair was brushed to the limits of its natural sheen and my skin nearly polished raw. The finishing touch? A crisp, brand new, freshly ironed, perfectly fitted white dress shirt. I showed up to this photo opportunity sharp as a tack, chest out, head back and extremely happy. We all struck our best poses and smiled brightly for the photograph. The black and white photograph. The irony of this aesthetic did not hit home until the paper with our picture was published. As I peeled back the pages in earnest anticipation, I was unprepared for the haunting image that burned a searing memory into my brain. There I stood, proud and stoic in my stark white shirt, while the darkness of my skin bled into the contrast of the paper, reducing my countenance to invisibility. As it turns out, my greatest indignation to date would exceed the rigors of reading, writing and arithmetic. For the first time in my life, I became aware of my dark skin. No, I was *made* aware of the darkness of my skin, in the cruelest way. In the days that followed, I prayed that I could fade into the featureless obscurity illustrated in that publication because the backlash from my peers was so insensitive I could not muster the strength to combat it, and my shame did not shield me from the abuse. I was humiliated. What should have been the proudest moment of my young life became the bane of my existence. A vicious introduction to the blinding pain of the mean-spirited and insulting nature of adults and children I not only considered my peers, but my friends.

It took weeks (perhaps years) before my mother and father were able to rebuild the confidence they instilled in me prior to that disastrous event. Dignity that took *years* to build was dismantled in a matter of a few malicious, hate-filled minutes.

Eventually, I regained my self-assurance. In fact, it came back so potently I had to temper it lest I be dubbed egotistical or narcissistic. I had to find a balance. And I did.

This was a difficult memory to revisit. So many years ago, and the experience still resonates. I am certain many of you can relate. Most of us have memories that dredge up a tinge of hurt when they skim the surface of our consciousness, which is ok as long as you focus less on the slight, betrayal or injustice and more on how far you have come since the experience. You are *still* standing. It did not break you, even if you thought you would never recover. That is a sign of strength. A sign you are bigger than your challenges. No, *proof* you are bigger than your challenges.

I went on to hold several offices throughout my academic career, including Student Council President, President of Fellowship of Christian Athletes, Choir President and Class President. I held each position proudly and used my scholarly success in the political arena to seed the path for the leadership roles I hold today. Do I wish I did not have to suffer such degradation? Sure. Do I regret the experience? Not one bit. It made me a better man. A more compassionate man. A more understanding man. Someone who can see a person in pain and say I have been there. I understand and have faith you will be fine. Friedrich Nietzsche wrote, "That which does not kill us, makes us stronger".[+] As long as you have the breath of life, you must believe that you have all you need to survive what life throws your way.

I do have one caveat: Some causes are not worth fighting for. You must also accept that you cannot win some of your battles. Had my mother behaved differently when asked to leave the diner, she might have paid dire consequences. She could have been kicked off the team, suspended or otherwise disciplined. She may have even been verbally assaulted. She had no rights at the time, and would have been fighting a losing battle. Sometimes, it is prudent to leave ego at the door so common sense can climb in through a window. Learn to pick your battles. Going with events as they are, even if you disagree with the premise and the possible outcome, does not mean you are submissive or condone the status quo. It means you took the time to think past the heat of the moment, considered all the potential effects of your actions, and you made a decision that works in your favor. When you came face to face with your cause, your adversity, you were strategic and tactical. Malcolm X observed, "There is no better than adversity. Every defeat, every heartbreak, every loss, contains its own seed, its own lesson on how to improve your performance the next time".

[+]   Friedrich Nietzsche "Twilight of the Idols", trans. R.J. Holingdale (Germany: C.G. Neuman, 1889)

Certificate of Congressional Recognition

Presented to

Carlos Wallace

On the Occasion of the

Top Ladies of Distinction, Inc., Sugar Valley Chapter

Annual Status of Women Scholarship Luncheon and Fashion Show

"Movers and Shakers - Making a Difference in the Community"

NOW THEREFORE BE IT RESOLVED that, on behalf of the constituents of the Eighteenth Congressional District of Texas, I take great pride in recognizing you has a Top Ladies of Distinction Inc. Honoree. You have impacted your community or people in your workplace in a positive way. Our lives belong to the whole community and as long as we live, it should be a privilege to do for it whatever we can. Indeed your willingness to give of yourself to your community is certainly deserving of the respect, admiration and commendation of the United States Congress.

May 5, 2012

Sheila Jackson Lee
Member of Congress

After my mother shared her story, I understood why I rarely saw her cry. Life's experiences wrung her pain dry. All she knew was how to hold back tears and fight. She told me that she was not alone in her struggle however. My grandfather, after hearing of her ordeal after the game, did what any doting father would. His little girl never travelled to any game without him ever again. She never ate alone in an empty school bus again. She behaved like a soldier on the field of battle. Her father showed her that she was not fighting the war alone.

My mother transferred her grit, her will to persevere amid the most disheartening circumstances to me, and the traits helped me heal after my painful encounter. Today, this mind-set is all I know. I hope to pass it on to you. That doggedness can be your armor; a shield you can wear against a world full of hostilities.

The sting of adversity hurts no matter who you are and it can emanate from several different sources. I think most of us know *someone* who criticizes to diminish our confidence or shake our faith. A co-worker, teacher, a friend or even a mate can project their insecurity in order to feel superior. Society is littered with a hateful lot who cast aspersions and spew bigotry, injustice and discord to demean and demoralize. Violators closest to us obviously know which buttons to push. They are privy to our vulnerabilities and know how to rattle us. You must learn how to steel yourself against life's acerbic realities in order to withstand such offenses. The reality is, people we love will die. We will encounter disappointment. People will hurt us. Life will not always be easy. We live, we learn. It is not my intention to over-simplify life's troubles. Personal responses to challenges are relative. I handle obstacles my way and I want you to learn how to use your own experiences to overcome difficulties in a manner that suits you.

Some people rise above challenges to overcome adversity. For others, overcoming adversity is an insurmountable challenge. Your way of thinking determines both attitudes. To those of us who subscribe to religious beliefs and look to God or a higher power to help us deal with adversity, I say this: you either have faith that you are highly favored or you block your favor because you lose faith. You cannot say that you place your trust in the will of God or a higher power *and* worry about everything at the same time. If you take your concerns to the proverbial altar, lay them there and walk away. I always say, you must bless and release in order for your blessings to be released!

From now on, as you face each day and meet with challenges, always remember: experience offers wisdom, it teaches, it guides. However, as Benjamin Disraeli wrote, "There is no education like Adversity". [5]

---

[5] Benjamin Disraeli, *Endymion* (London: Longmans & Green, 1880),

FEARLESS

Passive acceptance cripples our power. Working class people with a strong united voice, and supported by formidable leadership, pose a tremendous threat to companies that amass riches by hiding behind lax regulations and the arrogant assumption that we are too intimidated or uninformed to speak up.

V

Fearless. There is crushing power in that word. Stop for a moment and think about its meaning: *the absence of fear, brave.* Can you imagine how pleasant our lives would be if we made decisions, faced opposition and confronted each day without the paralyzing apprehension that often renders us powerless against adversity? How effortlessly we would take on our biggest problems if we were not limited by our fears?

In the previous chapter, I detailed the importance of dealing with adversity. Here, I want to share what I have found to be the one thing, the biggest detriment, to tackling your life head on: *overcoming fear.* Until we understand how fear trips us up on our journey through life, we will continue to exist in an arrested state of apprehension. Consequently, once we break free from this state, our entire approach to life is subject to improve exponentially. You can't beat adversity if you are too scared to get in the ring and fight.

Distress caused by self-doubt and fear of the unknown can be debilitating. When I realized just how much, I became determined to steel myself against its deleterious influence. You cannot, nor should you choose to, navigate your life shrouded in fear. This is not to suggest that you should not exercise caution and use common sense when making decisions. There is a difference between being brave and being reckless. I am also not implying that you will never be afraid. However, when fear goes unchecked, growth and progress stalls. Most times, we are petrified of the unknown. We fear an outcome we can't predict, much less assign a feeling to, fear or otherwise. Author and Spiritual Teacher Eckhart Tolle put it best: "The psychological condition of fear is divorced from any concrete and true immediate danger. It comes in many forms: unease, worry, anxiety, nervousness, tension, dread, phobia and so on. This kind of psychological fear is always of something that might happen, not of something that is happening now".[6]

History validates the undeniable and transformative influence of courageous people. Some examples that come to mind include: Dr. Martin Luther King, Jr., Malcolm X, Barack Obama, Mumia Abu Jamal, Marcus Garvey, Rosa Parks, Harriet Tubman, Booker T. Washington, John F. Kennedy, W.E.B. DuBois, Abraham Lincoln, Sojourner Truth and John Brown. All of these heroic figures, amid unspeakable opposition, refused to succumb to fear. Each opposed some form of oppression or another at great personal sacrifice. Whether it was from the pulpit or a podium, under the cover of dark tunnels or on a segregated bus, from behind prison bars or through the pages of books and essays, they helped us know freedom because fear was not an option.

There will come a time when you must be stronger than your challenges and insecurities. Each of us can be measured by our ability to rise above circumstances that threaten to hold us down. It is imperative that you draw a line fear cannot cross and remain obstinate. It was not until I suffered my most traumatic and life-altering circumstances did I come to realize the impact fear, if not checked, can have on our existence.

I doubt I will have to overcome an obstacle greater than dealing with the deaths of my parents and grandparents. My mother, who

---

[6]   Eckhart Tolle, *The Power of Now* (Canada: Namaste Publishing, 1997),

succumbed to complications from diabetes, was my best friend. My father, a hulking figure with a heart of gold, eternally redefined in my mind what it means to be a real man. Aaron Lee Wallace, Jr. was a consummate provider, a tireless worker and a pillar in our community. He was my hero. To this day, his example frames my character. I owe everything I am today to my mom, dad, grandfather and grandmother. As each of them left this earth, they took a piece of my soul with them and left a deep, bottomless void. To suggest that I was not scared when my loved ones died would be a fallacy of epic proportion. I *was* afraid. It was as if I was wandering aimlessly through what remained of my life.

That is, until one day, a moment of clarity. As I sat alone recounting the memories that held me together as much as they ripped me apart, I understood that I was behaving contrary to what these special people taught me. My mother became a prominent, successful educator despite being a single mom for three years after leaving an abusive husband. She could have retreated into a shell and become overly cautious and reclusive. Instead, she cast her trepidations aside. She was fearless. My father married my mother, knowing she had a young son and a crippling illness, and loved her eternally. He could have listened to naysayers who warned the so-called baggage this woman was carrying would be a burden. He took a daring step. He was fearless. My grandfather defied racist opposition and segregationist mandates during one of the most deplorable periods in our nation's history to become the honorable Judge O'Neal Hunt. He was fearless. My grandmother, who I affectionately called "Mubba", stood by him, unwavering and stoic. She was a nurturing homemaker and life partner. Fearless. I was- and I still am- my parent's son and Granddaddy's and Mubba's pride and joy. I owed it to them to carry on their legacies and reflect their strength. I needed to conquer my challenges as they had conquered theirs. I owed it to them to be fearless. When I finally began coping with their deaths and the pall of foreboding that hung over my now solitary life lifted, I understood that there was no limit to my resolve.

Somewhere, someone in your life embodies a fearlessness you can tap. That person may even be you! Every time you stood up for something you believed in, locked horns with confrontation, stood toe to toe with adversity, you set aside fear and claimed your life back from the destructive hold of a self-imposed dread. FDR once said, "We have nothing to fear but fear itself".[7] Today, make a conscious choice; do not allow trepidation to keep you from happiness or success.

My professional life has been a true test of my mettle. Over the years, I have had to siphon fresh reserves of patience and strength to fend off menacing bouts of the fear I work so hard to keep at bay.

My life, in a nutshell, has been filled with waves of grace marked by undercurrents of mercilessness. The good and the bad. I am a fifth generation railroader. I state this proudly every opportunity I can, because I find that, these days, we rarely hear of families that can claim a common vocation that spans generations. I am also the Founder and President of a successful entertainment company, Sol-Caritas. The uncommon name, which is Latin for "elite giving", raised eyebrows at first. I was surprised at how many people predicted the company would fail simply because they felt no one would understand the name. Thankfully, these predictions never came to pass. Today, Sol is on its way to becoming a household name and one of the premier management and promotions companies in the country *(waves of grace)*. I launched Sol with the support of good friends. Everyone contributed their expertise to help establish my life's blood. I tapped the talents of friends who were proficient in marketing, the internet, public relations and writing. I ventured into the world of social media and in less than three years built an explosive fan base.

---

[7]   Franklin D. Roosevelt "The Only Thing We Have to Fear is Fear Itself" (speech, First Presidential Inaugural Address of Franklin D. Roosevelt, Washington, D.C. March 4, 1933)

The main reason I established the business was to create a source of income. My family and I needed a means to subsist after I was fired for over three years without pay (*undercurrent of mercilessness*). You want to talk about being terrified! For a man, not being able to support his family may be one of the most disquieting predicaments. Following a thorough investigation, I was reinstated in good standing and my service record remains flawless. Still, the battle was over but the war raged on.

In the years that followed my dismissal, I rose through the ranks in the union (*waves of grace*). Nevertheless, with each nomination, I felt the sting of racism. With each appointment, I was reminded that no matter how qualified I was for the position, I was still nothing more than a black man. I choose not to use the more pejorative derivative of the terms used to describe me (*undercurrent of mercilessness*).

In 2013, at the encouragement of my union's leadership and trusted colleagues and business associates, I entered a rather contentious race (the last one of my union career) for a coveted position as a Chairman. I understood the challenge before me and remained aware of the undercurrent of dissent and racial tension. However, I was qualified for the position and that was all that mattered to me.

Throughout the race, some of my union brothers and sisters expressed concerns about my age, my company and my race. It became evident that despite the strides we have made in bridging the racial divide, we may never completely erase the memory of one of the darkest times in our nation's history, a stain the fabric of our diverse nation. Bear in mind, I was neither offended nor deterred by this reality. What *did* upset me was seeing the men and women who stood with me on the front lines of fierce negotiations and amid perilous conditions turn on me. They were afraid that backing me would jeopardize their standing in the union. It was not because they doubted my ability. They just did not want to be associated with me if the election did not fare in our favor. They would say, "I'd side with you Carlos, and I know you are the best man for the job, but if you lose I don't want the appointed leader to hold it against me". My heart fell. I realized that despite the sacrifices our forefathers made so that we could stand firm and united, these men and women were afraid to speak up for what is right. They were afraid to claim something for the better good. They were simply, afraid.

It was not unlike any other obstacle I faced over the course of my life. Perhaps the only difference was I was older, wiser and certainly much more resilient. As fate would have it, those characteristics served as the armor I would need to withstand the outcome of the election. It did not fare in my favor. I lost by a landslide. And as I stood face to face with the reality and was reminded that past is prologue when it comes to race relations in corporate America, I remained stoic.

I am nothing if not a man of conviction. I am a die-hard Democrat, win or lose. I am a loyal Cowboy's fan, win or lose. I am a life-long Lakers fan, win or lose. In addition, I am a tried and true union man, win or lose. I respect everyone who do not agree with my affiliations and steadfastly uphold their own choices. In life, you have to pick a side and defend it to the end. Sometimes, you may stand alone as I did so often in a union that boasted equality for all. I have to admit, nothing is scarier than believing you are surrounded by an army, only to realize you are on a solo mission fighting for your life. Still, I may have stood alone, but I maintained my dignity. I maintained my respect for the industry, despite my trials. I was fearless.

There is freedom attached to knowing you fought the good fight. When you know your did not deviate from your convictions and beliefs, you have peace of mind. If you could learn to set aside feelings of victimization and the misguided inference that everyone is out to persecute you or keep you from succeeding, you are already a winner.

If you learn that you are capable of determining the course of your life, I will be satisfied that this chapter, this book, will not have been in vain.

To know who you are is a source of great power. You are shielded from the debilitating effects of insecurity and doubt. You walk more proudly, stand taller, make better decisions, and take control of your destiny. Furthermore, I understand that to lead is a privilege, not an entitlement. It does not make you better than anyone; it helps you bring out the best in everyone. Accolades do not inspire a real leader's vision because they have set their sights on the success of others. Leaders bypass shortsightedness and focus on the big picture. Leaders who always stand righteously never stand alone. They are honorable. They are committed. They are enduring. They are fearless.

Following the election, the only people who were upset or disappointed were those who did not support me because they were afraid. They allowed others to tarnish the image of their "Golden Boy". Fortunately, for my sake and sanity, that image never defined me. The disparaging opinions of others did not level me. In fact, I was motivated to carry on with the next phase of my professional and personal life. I dedicated more time and effort to my business and my family. I found great satisfaction in knowing that my success with both was measured by positive results and that eventually credit was given where it was due. I still work to make a difference and to improve the status quo. My personal goals and priorities present unlimited occasion for growth. George Bernard Shaw wrote, "The reasonable man adapts himself to the world, the unreasonable one persists in trying to adapt the world to himself. Therefore all progress depends on the unreasonable man".[8] I realize that some people may consider some

---

[8]   George Bernard Shaw, *Man and Superman* (USA: Penguin Classics, 2001),

of my decisions *unreasonable.* In the case of the election and most of my personal choices, based on Mr. Shaw's observations, that assessment is quite fitting.

Most times, it's not that we can't, it's that we will not or we are too afraid to try. Fear limits us. Uncertainty limits us. Doubt limits us. We have to get out of own way, in order to reach our chosen destination. As we make our way toward our goals, we will face challenges. We will face loss. We will encounter change. We will be forced to adapt. It is never one straight shot from point A to point Z on the road to success. If you think that is the case, you are setting yourself up for disappointment. Accept that obstacles are a reality, and you will be better equipped to deal with them. Finally, if have difficulty handling adversity, focus on building your emotional and mental fortitude. Focus on being Fearless.

DISAPPOINTMENT

To some, it seems success comes easily. But few realize how much disappointment, rejection, frustration, uncertainty and pressure it takes to get there. It's ok to hunger for your desired dream. But you must be willing to shed a few pounds of flesh in order to someday feast off the fruits of your labor!

VI

Disappointment. Yes, we have to talk about it. In order to get a better understanding of how we complicate our lives, we must acknowledge that this demoralizing feeling is an unavoidable reality. While the purpose of this book is to inspire and uplift, to achieve that end we must explore the darkest recesses of our essential nature. Fortunately, this is a journey we can take together.

Disappointment is a tie that binds. If you think about it, it is one of few things most, if not all of us have in common simply because we have all experienced disappointment in some form. Whether you were devastated by the loss of a loved one, distraught after being rejected by an employer, frustrated your child is not living up to your expectations, or distressed because your relationship failed, chances are you have been felled by disappointing circumstances. I've been there. More times than I care to count. And let's face it, this is a feeling we all would love to avoid. However we need to deal with disappointment and its effects head on. Life becomes less complicated when you do.

I will not insult your intelligence by reiterating a concept you may have heard

hundreds of times. We are all perfectly aware that the way we maneuver life's peaks and valleys determines how we endure its challenges. You may be inclined to believe that this is easier said than done. On the contrary. Forasmuch as you cannot predict if and when you will be disappointed, once it happens you have only two choices: You can either let it consume you, until you become bitter and resentful. Or, you can accept what has happened, learn from it and move on. It really is that simple. What we tend to do is over analyze. We replay the circumstances over and over again, trying to extrapolate "Why me", "why now", "what if"? And while answers to these questions may bring you some peace of mind, it will not change the circumstances that disappointed you to begin with. Nothing will. What you can change is how long you empower the feeling. One of my favorite authors, Eckhart Tolle said, "The primary cause of unhappiness is never the situation but thought about it. Be aware of the thoughts you are thinking. Separate them from the situation, which is always neutral. It is as it is."[9] In my experience, the sooner you let it go, the sooner you heal. There are so few circumstances in life that require no guesswork whatsoever. Deciding you want your life back after a being disappointed, is one of those times. That greatly limits the complexity!

One of the greatest misconceptions about me is that I lead a charmed life; I don't have a care in the world. That could not be farther from the truth! Please don't misunderstand. I am blessed beyond measure in more ways than I can accurately innumerate in one book. However I have faced my fair share of disappointment, many times by people closest to me. I have been deceived, betrayed, taken advantage of, maligned; friends and family have stolen from

---

9   Eckhart Tolle, *Awakening to Your Life's Purpose* (USA: Plume, 2006),

me, jeopardized my reputation and tried to undermine me more times than I care to remember. And of course I asked myself how people I trusted and who claimed they loved me could be so cruel? But no matter what the answer, it did not undo the offense. Dwelling on the situation is like walking through drying cement; eventually you get stuck. Permanently. Instead, I chose to address the issue. I made a mental note, picked myself up and continued living my life. Yes, I was hurt. Yes, I was confused. Of course I was disappointed. But I had a plan in mind for my life and I could not let the insidious actions of other people take me off course. There was no reason to. I was doing the right thing, pursuing my goals, fulfilling my mission one day at a time. I take care of my children, provide for my family, and run a successful business. I am charitable, generous and kind. I had done nothing wrong. So why would I risk all that, to reward the negative intention of others with more of my valuable time than necessary?

The answer is I would not. And you shouldn't either. You control the effect people have over you in literally every aspect of your life. This is your greatest power. You choose to say, you can't hurt me. You choose to say, I won't let you mistreat me. You choose to say I am not going to dwell in another person's negative space. No one can keep you where you do not want to be. They may put you there for a brief time, but the decision to open the door, walk out and lock it behind you is solely your own.

Today, I have a very tight knit, very small circle of friends and family. My best friends John John, Lorenza and Vinson and I have been thick as thieves since we were 3 years old. My boy Cody, who I met while in college is the epitome of loyalty and support. I also make it a point to surround myself with other positive people who I trust hold my best interests in as high regard as I hold theirs. People who have proven their loyalty. Disappointment taught me early that every now and then it is prudent to reevaluate my social sphere and that I should protect my personal life vigilantly. I reveal this for one important reason: to remind anyone reading these words that no matter how put together a person may look on the outside, sometimes there are mental and emotional scars buried deep beneath the surface.

When you look at people that appear to have it all together, it is not necessarily because they lead such an easy life. It's because they choose not to be distracted by unfortunate circumstances they can not change. They would rather focus on the things they can change. It is more important to fix the situation than it is to become fixated on it. People who take control, rather than allow themselves to be controlled will always prevail. I urge you to challenge your enemies, instead of being challenged by them. Victims will never be victorious. They are too vulnerable; they are open wounds that allow the infectious nature of others to poison their thinking.

We have only to look beyond our personal feelings about a person or action in order to discover a lesson. There will be days you wonder "Why did this person hurt me?" or "Why did I lose my job right when I am struggling the most?" or "Why is my child giving me such a hard time?" You may never be able to understand the actions of others, but you absolutely can control your reaction. I had no clue why my parents would lay the burden of paying a bill in our household on my shoulders (at eleven, this was like moving the rock of Gibraltar). But, I did not question them. I did what I had to do in order to make the situation work for me. Finding out later that there was a method to their thinking that transcended anything I would have surmised, affirms that taking the high road benefited everyone.

When faced with such uncertainty, or painful experiences, you must do your best to look beyond the actual event. Focus on your role in the experience. Think it out. Ask yourself how can I prevail, how can I make this work in my favor, how can I turn this around.

No matter how angry you are about being mistreated or slighted, you will not change the fact that it happened. Therefore, it will only behoove you to make it work for you. If you lose your job, do not wallow. Wallowing never paid the mortgage. Tap into your strengths and think of ways to make ends meet while you work on getting another full-time job. If your kids are misbehaving, teach them hard life lessons. Stop asking what you did wrong and tell them in no uncertain terms why their behavior is not right. That may mean denying them the little extras they feel they are entitled to and showing them that if they want something, they have to earn it with good behavior. Take control. You are the parent. My mom never asked me if I wanted to pay the cable bill. She told me to do it. If I wanted to live there, I had to fall in line.

If you can train yourself to be actionable instead of reactionary, you will break out of the negative space that is typically furnished with fear, uncertainty and inaction, and move into that peaceful zone of determination, power, decisiveness and growth.

This is why it is so important to arm yourself with the belief you control your destiny no matter what happens around you. When I worked as a Corrections Officer on Death Row of the Texas Department of Corrections – Institutions Division, it never ceased to amaze me, how some of these men, sentenced to die, refused to let their circumstances weigh them down. They use to say, "C.O. Wallace, as long as I have breath, I have hope". Truth of the matter is, most clarity follows the darkest moments. That's just the way it is. Think about it . . .when was the last time you were feeling completely confident and everything was going as planned, and thought to yourself euphorically "there is a lesson here! I understand"? I mean it's possible to have those "Aha" moments while basking in the glow of contentment, but typically it happens after we've been knocked around a bit and we are emotionally, spiritually and physically exhausted by the very prospect of another minute of hopelessness. We bounce around, feeling our way through difficult issues, navigating complex relationships, gaining a better understanding of self through emotion and reason. The good thing is (well, it's more than good; it's actually critical to growth and enlightenment), every experience, interaction, conversation (yes, even the negative ones) has a valuable lesson within. Sometimes the revelation is within reach; other times we have to look deeper. Here's the key, and the realization that frightens a lot of us; we must be willing to see, hear, listen and accept what we learn about ourselves (which is not always pretty) and about how we relate to others and life in general. Still, when the lesson manifests itself make sure you *seriously, carefully* consider the message and make the necessary changes so the difficult journey to this answer was not in vain. With that kind of positive thinking, there is absolutely no room for Disappointment.

DELIVERANCE

People are who they are. The personalities of most adults have been etched by years of victories and disappointments, joys and sorrows. You can't change anyone nor should you try. Embrace what is good, and accept you will not like everything about them. If you love them try to find balance. No one is perfect. In the end, the only thing you have control over, is you and how you choose to deal with others.

VII

While compiling research for this book, I referred to my favorite authors and academics. I read books by Don Miguel Ruiz, Joel Osteen, Eckhart Tolle, and Deepak Chopra. I examined poetry by Dr. Maya Angelou, Langston Hughes, and Nikki Giovani. I studied the tragedies of Shakespeare and the detailed epics of Toni Morrison. I reflected on the teachings of the Bible, my most valuable resource. I did all this because I knew that in order to fully understand and convey what I have come to learn about human nature and about myself, and if I want to help others conquer seemingly insurmountable challenges, I had to study experts that mastered a comprehension of pure, raw emotion and explored the deepest recess of a person's psyche. Without this knowledge, I would have been unable to write this chapter. Moreover, I would not have been able to assist someone close to me.

Just when you think you are so set in your ways that nothing, and no one, can change one ounce of your personality, you learn that sometimes you have to give a little in order to gain so much more. I am a firm believer that you should never try to alter a person's character to suit your needs. People are who they are. If you are not happy with someone, perhaps he or she is not the one for you. This holds true for significant others, friends and even co-workers. I am not suggesting that you quit your job in order to ditch dealing with a colleague. However, do your best to separate business matters from personal interaction. Now, if you have an open mind and are able and willing to communicate your concerns, well this creates a different scenario. Giving that one inch can make a world of difference. Sometimes it can also reveal things about others and yourself that can alter your life.

I know I have said this before, but you never really know a person's story. We are all works in progress. Sadly, the most troubled among us are those who do not recognize their faults and limitations, yet are quick to point out what they consider frailties in other people. These tortured souls are hard to identify because they *seem* perfect on the outside. However, they are as flawed as the next person is. By the way, never believe anyone is better off than you based on appearances. What seems "put together" on the surface could be quite unsettled within.

I believe one of the greatest blessings God has granted me (and there are quite a few) is my ability and willingness to learn from all I observe, encounter or experience. I say this is a blessing because far too often we focus so much on our own lives, we overlook the needs and wants of those closest to us. I am not suggesting this is a bad thing. Acute attention to one's life is part of the journey toward self-fulfillment. I am just pointing out that if we fail to look beyond what is right under our nose we may miss an opportunity to understand and help someone whose pain lies beneath the surface. Case in point: a stunning revelation from one of my best friends unleashed a reality check so powerful, it sent shockwaves through my emotions, and I am *not* an emotional person. The epiphany redefined our friendship.

It occurred about a time that I noticed he was just not himself. Typically gregarious and affable, there was something a little off about his behavior. He seemed disconnected and uncharacteristically sad. I had not seen him in some time and just assumed he just had a lot on his mind. He was just promoted to a management position, recently bought a new house and had been blessed with a new child. That's enough to make anyone a little stressed out.

One evening, I received a disturbing phone call. The bartender at a local spot my buddy and I frequented, especially during football season, urged me to come immediately because my friend was dangerously intoxicated and insisted on driving home. I promptly beat a path to our hangout, confused and concerned that someone I would trust with my life, had obviously lost all regard for his own. Back in college, if anyone had exhibited this kind of behavior, this guy would have read them the riot act. Recklessness was never part of his repertoire. When I arrived, I pressed him for an explanation. I was hoping it was something as simple as stress from work or a misunderstanding at home. I could not have been more mistaken. He sobered up a bit, and we talked. I found out why his behavior had become so erratic. The revelation hit me like a freight train. He admitted that for much of his adult life, he suffered from clinical depression, and the illness had become unmanageable. The blank stare on my face clearly said it all. I had my very first, personal introduction to this crippling illness.

Some of you may be wondering, "What is the big deal? So, what, he was depressed?" Well, it was not so much hearing that he was depressed. It was knowing that this man, who never showed weakness, sadness or frustration, had a vulnerability. Yet, despite that vulnerability, he was *still* the same great person. My perception about how people handle issues and difficult situations needed an upgrade. On some level an overhaul! You see, I was raised to believe nothing is insurmountable. I tackle issues head on, without complaints or wallowing in despair. I have a deep-seated urge to find the positive in every situation. And here was a man who had a great job, who was educated, raised in a good home, had an extraordinary family. By all accounts, this was the ideal individual. How could he find a reason to be unhappy? What could be that bad? It seemed inconceivable to me that he could not appreciate how good he had it! However, I was judging him based on a condition I did not understand. I was not familiar with the illness therefore I reacted as most people do; I expected pep talks and tough love (and a night out) to "snap him out of it". After we talked though, I began to shed my preconceived notions and took the time to learn more about this medical condition.

It was important for me to write about this experience, because I now know depression is a very common form of mental illness. You never know who may be suffering with the condition. Because of the stigma attached, you may never realize that mood swings, constant unhappiness and feelings of despair belie a very serious chemical imbalance. By not telling me right away, he did not give me the information I needed to understand or help him. I could not have his back because I did not know what he was facing. As it turns out, we helped each other. I took a step back and admitted I needed to be a more understanding person; I needed to be less "black and white" in my approach to life and people. The realization was so liberating. It was sincerely a moment of mental and emotional deliverance. I was emancipated from a state of mind that threatened to hold me back.

I cannot help but think O'Neal Hunt would have been proud of his grandson. He always taught me that sometimes you have to look beyond what you've always known in order to help a friend discover something worth knowing. He discovered that he did not have to fight the illness alone. I now understand that even the strongest among us (including me) can succumb to circumstances beyond our control, and that is ok.

Today, I am very sensitive about depression and its effects. I summarily address those who incorporate the "diagnosis" to describe less severe feelings without respecting how seriously this illness affects the lives of so many people. Having a bad day does not make you depressed. Being sad your team lost does not make you depressed. A flash of frustration or short-term sadness does not necessarily qualify as depression.

According to the National Institute of Mental Health, symptoms of depression may include the following:

- Difficulty concentrating, remembering details, and making decisions
- Fatigue and decreased energy
- Feelings of guilt, worthlessness, and/or helplessness
- Feelings of hopelessness and/or pessimism
- Insomnia, early-morning wakefulness, or excessive sleeping
- Irritability, restlessness
- Loss of interest in activities or hobbies once pleasurable, including sex
- Overeating or appetite loss
- Persistent aches or pains, headaches, cramps, or digestive problems that do not ease even with treatment
- Persistent sad, anxious, or "empty" feelings
- Thoughts of suicide, suicide attempts

If you think you or someone you care about may be exhibiting signs of depression, I urge you to seek professional assistance as soon as possible. Talk with someone about your feelings. You are not alone.

Today, if you do not do anything else, make a list of your lifelines. People or activities you can turn to that give you an extra push or added motivation. The goal is to build your mental, spiritual and physical fortitude so the "bad days" do not creep up on you as often or linger too long. Before you know it, if you actively practice thinking more positively (operative word here is practice), you will find living in that "happy place" is so much more fulfilling. It is critical that you focus on the people (and activities) that make you happy. We can make as many excuses as we would like to explain why we wallow in bouts of misery but (if we are honest with ourselves) we know . . .it is a choice. Plain and simple. I know that some choices are much more difficult than others are. And some "sadness" requires special attention. Ultimately, the final arbiter of how you live your life is you. You do not have to associate with negative people. You do not have to be caught up in "drama". You do not have to hold that grudge. You do not have to "hate". You do not have to be with someone who does not value you. You do not have to tolerate or do a single thing that does not encourage peace, and calm, and contentment in your life. We are such powerful beings! In addition, we are guided and protected by an Almighty Creator. Imagine the things we could do and the thoughts that would prevail, and the comforting feelings that would wash over us if we remained faithful and accepted how much we are in control of our lives! You must get right with you in order to do what is right for you. Most times, it is not the world or people around us that are in chaos or causing turmoil. That confusion often comes from within. Take a moment, take a breath, and take the time you need to know yourself. Take control. Speak love and kindness into your own heart. Stop looking for external remedies to cure your internal pain.

Be still. Quiet the noise. Listen. Embrace how absolutely, positively, incontrovertibly amazing you are, and live your life accordingly.

In the end, it is so important to remain encouraged, and to be a source of encouragement, and to know that in your darkest moments God has provided you with light. That light is your friends. That light is your circle of loved ones. That light is that voice within that reminds you, no matter how badly you may feel now you will heal. You will overcome. Sometimes, the light comes when -and from someone- you least expect. That's God making his presence known. Do not suffer in silence. You must always make sure the lines of communication are wide open and accept your light is within reach. Sometimes it is just a phone call away.

In addition, when you can, be the light someone else may need. Listen to your heart, be selfless, heal a friend and embrace the signs that may some day put them on a healing course toward Deliverance.

VALIDATION

Truth is, living up to people's expectations limits your potential. You will find that they are unreasonably high, or set so low you should consider it an insult. Be your own bar. Decide how you will reach your goal. Then no one can lay claim to your success. Do not worry about meeting the standard when you are the standard.

VIII

Shakespeare's *Hamlet* has been described as one of the most profound, complex and prolific literary works and is probably the most famous play in the English language. As with many of Shakespeare's dramas, the characters and their conflicts withstood the test of time and for many, mirror present-day life. So many of us can relate to the hero's dilemma in *Hamlet*; his struggle with two opposing forces: moral integrity and the desire to avenge his father's murder. Think about how many times you and I struggle with our own inner conflicts? Those moments when we search our souls for the right decisions about life, family and love. Scared to death that the choices we make will possibly change our lives.

I have been torn on occasion between making the right decision and choosing the option that I know will make me delirious with satisfaction. If you smiled at the latter then we are on the same page. That choice we think will bring us the sweet taste of vindication probably involves someone being on the receiving end of cosmic retribution. Therefore, I think it is safe to say, we have all lived through our own personal Hamlet at one time or another. While one can extract a wealth of philosophical truths from this famous play, for the sake of this book I will reference one of Shakespeare's wisest pronouncements on living a peaceful life: "This above all: to thine own self be true."[10] These are words to live by every single day.

Of all the things I have desired in my lifetime, (success, happiness, love, respect), thankfully the validation of others has never been among them. I possess the prodigious ability to be indifferent to the opinion of others. This attitude could be mistaken as me being aloof. As a matter of fact when I explain this aspect of my personality to people I am getting to know -and even to those whom I have been friends with for some time- they often suggest I am unfeeling or narcissistic. That is not the case.

I live to honor the memory of my parents, my grandparents and my uncle Rube Earl, who was one of my best friends up until the day he died. In order to do so, I have to be aware of how I am perceived by those closest to me and by business partners, colleagues and clients. My family would settle for nothing less than respectability, integrity, discipline kindness and compassion. And for the most part, I believe I comply.

What I do not do is kowtow to those who disagree with my opinions or my life simply because it differs from their own. I do not live my life to please others and neither should you. This does not make you arrogant. This simply allows you to determine who you are without being sidetracked by what outsiders think you should be. Everyone needs this assuredness or else they risk constantly second-guessing themselves, their goals and even their lives. Only you can decide what is in your best interest and pandering to the interests of others will only impede your progress.

---

[10] William Shakespeare, *The Complete Works of Shakespeare, Fifth Edition*, David Bevington, ed. Longman, 2003.

This confidence actually allows me to maintain complex relationships. Experience has shown me that you will always fare better in life and with others when you know, trust and follow your own mind. Great freedom stems from the realization you absolutely do not have to be bound by what people think about you and your decisions. It reinforces self-confidence and encourages you to think beyond the boundaries of the status quo. It is empowering, comforting and the best way to protect the delicate sensibilities that leave a person's feelings exposed and vulnerable.

Do most people prefer to be liked? Well sure! But realistically, not everyone is going to like you and you will not always please everyone. Therefore, it is important for you to reach a level of self-awareness and confidence that will offset some of the resistance you may face. Appreciate the accolades but do not be disillusioned by the critics. Find a healthy median and realize that neither should be the final arbiter of who you are.

Some people live most of their lives with a crippling need to be liked and accepted by everyone. Yes, I said everyone. I have friends who know, lets say, 100 people. Ninety-nine adore them. The one person they cannot reach becomes an obsession; it could be a colleague or an audience member at a comedy show, or in the case of one friend who is a t-v anchor, a viewer who does not like her hair or outfit one day. One negative assessment completely offsets any positive feedback. Suffice it to say engaging that stream of consciousness wears them out. One friend admitted that some days her brain would just about short circuit as she tried to decipher why she could not tickle the fancies of that select few. It took a toll on her mood and health as well.

Another great drawback with this way of thinking is, while you are busy focusing on your critics, you are discounting the people who appreciate you. More importantly, you are overlooking the only person whose opinion frames your life: You. It is irrational to give people you barely know, or who have no interest in your life, control over your moods. Some days, it might behoove us all to ask, "How can it be that I, an adult, cannot succeed in life because someone won't let me? Whether it is your boss, a family member or someone you are in a relationship with, no one can prevent you from accomplishing great things but you! The same power you give to people that you claim hold you back, use to knock them out of your way!

Furthermore, while the unfavorable judgments of a few should not disappoint you, the flattery of many (while fantastic) should not delight you. In other words opinions, good or bad, should not influence your state of mind. Remember, the more you have to proclaim how great, smart, talented and desirable people say you are, the less you truly believe it. Braggers project to quiet their insecurity. Humility is a restrained expression of your finest qualities. Humble confidence lets your best speak for itself.

This self-assuredness can only come if your inner-voice is the loudest. Your thoughts should be free flowing and uninterrupted by the musings of unsolicited commentators. The best way to accomplish that is to set up filters; a metaphorical mental fortress that separates what you hear from the receptors in your brain. Moreover, make sure the only person who controls what stimuli penetrate that fortress is you.

The power of mind over matter must be developed over time. Strengthened like a muscle. You have to learn how to trust your own judgment, follow your instincts and act on your own accord. It is not only mental. There must be a balance of mind, body and heart. You must learn to understand why you need the validation and acceptance of others in order to exist. That is a journey only you can take and questions only you can answer. The big risk you take with deep reflection is, you may not like the answers that rise to the surface. Still it is better to walk in clarity than it is to stumble aimlessly in darkness. If you are willing to delve deeply and sift through the noise, clutter, restlessness, pain and uncertainty taking up space within you, you will eventually find answers. Only then will you be able to deal with your issues. When you resurface, you will have such peace.

I have a feeling, if we treated most people exactly the way they treat us, they would learn to be *a lot* nicer. If we turn the tables instead of turning the other cheek, the bitter taste of someone's own medicine could prove the best cure for bad behavior. Contrarily, killing them with kindness could bury undesirable actions as well. In order to avoid confrontation or "take the high road" we have grown accustomed to brushing off bad or unkind behavior or making excuses for an individual's inconsiderate tendencies. Give people enough leeway to treat you poorly, they will take full advantage. Why shouldn't they? Some folks are prepared to do anything they can get away with, especially if in the end it suits their sensibilities.

Bottom line is, nasty is nasty. Rude is rude. Disrespect is disrespect, any way you look at it. If you choose to engage those who conduct themselves in this manner, you have pretty much handed them the keys to your inner peace and declared, "Please, wreak havoc on my mental and emotional stability!" Your best recourse? Take (or better yet, take back) complete ownership of your feelings. Demand respect and enforce that requisite consistently.

You may believe you need to conform to others. Untrue. The flip side is that people do not *have* to conform to you. We are ultimately beholden to ourselves. Now, the people who care (and matter)? Well, they will respect us for whom we are and conduct themselves accordingly, compromising when they need to because you are worth it. And so should we. As Sophocles taught, "Kindness is ever the begetter of kindness."

Ultimately, it is about claiming your power. I am not suggesting you shut everyone out. You need input sometimes, especially from people you trust. The beauty of listening to people's advice and opinions is you choose what to hear, absorb, and possibly take into consideration. You also determine what to discard.

Eleanor Roosevelt said "No one can make you feel inferior without your consent."[11] There comes a time, in everyone's life, where you must stop caring what everyone else thinks, what someone else is saying, and how other people feel about how you choose to live or you will go insane. We cannot call ourselves adults or masters of our own destiny if we are always looking for people to co-sign our every move. It is hard enough meeting your OWN expectations sometimes. Why add the burden of trying to reach those people who either do not have their own life together. or a genuine interest in your well being? Just be who you are. Now when you decide that you are strong enough to take that path, own it. Be responsible for the decision. If you are not willing to accept the person you have chosen to be, in any form, you certainly cannot expect others to. Draw the line and walk it, proudly. That is your greatest Validation.

---

[11] Eleanor Roosevelt, *This Is My Story* (New York: Garden City, 1939),

FREEDOM

Most clarity follows the darkest moments. We bump around, feeling our way through difficult issues, gaining a better understanding of self through emotion and reason. Every experience, interaction, conversation has a lesson within. Sometimes the revelation is within reach; other times we must look deeper. When it manifests itself, make sure you seriously, carefully consider the message, so the difficult journey toward this answer was not in vain.

IX

Freedom. Depending on whom you ask, the word can mean many things. I believe our broad understanding of the concept of freedom is as comprehensive as the word itself. Literally, freedom is defined as *an absence of limitations whether it is in choice, speech, religion or political affiliation.* I find that description to be too rigid and confining to do the word justice. Personally, I regard freedom as one of the most fluid, liberating and empowering motivators any one person can enjoy. Ultimately, it allows us to live an unburdened and largely uncomplicated life. To some, it seems freedom comes easily. However, few realize how much disappointment, rejection, frustration and pressure it takes to get to this state of mental and emotional salvation. Do not be deterred by that caveat. It is all right and quite essential to hunger and break a sweat for anything you desire. Passion for something you desire is a potent catalyst. However, you must be willing to shed a few pounds of flesh in order to someday feast off the fruits of your labor.

Inasmuch as there are varied interpretations of what freedom is and how it can be attained, I will speak from my personal experience in order to demonstrate that the sublime, life-affirming results this ethos promises can be found in the most unlikely (and sometimes tragic) circumstances. When we are done with this chapter, some of you may discover you are searching for freedom, or something like it, in all the wrong places.

By now, you are aware of the immeasurable influence my parents and grandparents had, and continue to have, on my life. To say that their tutelage was utterly transformative would be an understatement. I listened, I watched, I absorbed those lessons every day of my life. From the moment I could form -and retain- a cognitive, sensible stream of thought I began storing valuable gems that I would one day polish off and invest in myself in order to survive difficult moments. And believe me, their edification flowed. It is as if their knowledge and wisdom were connected to a spigot and by simply asking a question or paying very close attention, I released a flood of both in abundant supply.

Granddaddy, Mubba, Momma, Daddy; they were all demonstrably practical, straightforward, resolute and courageous even as they stared down their own mortality. *Especially* as they stared down their mortality.

My mother battled diabetes her entire life. To see her in action, you would never know that this athletic, dynamic, outspoken educator was at the mercy of this debilitating illness. And just as there will be those who knew my mother and may not believe how sick she was, more still will now learn that she chose on some level not to accept it. Call it denial, pride, obstinacy, or bravery; my mother carried on with her life as if she were the picture of vitality and had signed a perpetual contract with God. That sometimes meant not giving her delicate health the care it needed. Suffice it to say, diabetes proved to be a formidable opponent. My mother never stood a chance. In her final days, I watched the merciless disease rob me of the woman I knew. A pillar of strength reduced to a frail shell. Her once sharp mind blunted by medication and pain as complications from the diabetes ran their course, forcing her to lapse in and out of comas.

Yet, I held out hope that she would win this battle as she had so many others. One evening, after she had regained some semblance of awareness following a state of prolonged unconsciousness she found me standing in the spot where I had all but dug a permanent indentation into the ground; the space right at her hospital bedside. I noticed a glimmer in her eyes that I had been missing dearly and I was heartened. Her weak but beautiful smile enveloped me with warmth I can still feel today. It was visceral. She went on and on about how happy she would be to finally leave the hospital and her pain behind. "Baby, I can't wait to go home," she would say repeatedly. One day, she asked me to bring her favorite fleece blanket to stave off the clinical chill typical of all hospital rooms. Of course, I complied. When I visited the following day, I turned the corner to make my way down the long stark corridor. Before I could enter the now all too familiar room, the nurse usually on duty met me at the door. It was not hard to interpret the funereal look on her face. I knew immediately my mother, my best friend was gone.

Nelson Mandela is probably one of the greatest examples of freedom lost, and freedom won. The South African anti-apartheid revolutionary and politician served 27 years in prison, jailed for his efforts to end the oppression of apartheid. In his autobiography *Long Walk to Freedom* Mandela writes, "For to be free is not merely to cast off one's chains, but to live in a way that respects and enhances the freedom of others".[12] I can say without hesitation, my father is the personification of those words. My dad was one of the wisest men I have ever known and he played an integral role in shaping my philosophy on life. His influence was felt from the moment he embraced me as his son. My dad taught me how to ride a bike when I was four, drive a car when I was 14 and how to drive a train when I was 24. We were even roommates for a while when I first hired for the railroad. This was his way of making himself available while I became acclimated to my new career. Always a mentor, I stayed with him as I trained to be an engineer so he could teach me all about the railroad lifestyle and help me prepare for the task before me. As a fifth generation railroader, I welcomed the benefit of his extensive first-hand experience. During that time, I absorbed a valuable supply of insight. He had this knack for turning anything into a lesson. He would tell me often: "Everybody can teach you something son. Hell, you can even learn from a bum! If nothing else, he can show you that you do not want to be a bum!"

My Dad simply believed you should accept life at face value. There was no need for all the complicated and sometimes convoluted reasoning that so many of us get lost in. I agree that sometimes we over think a situation so much we end up undervaluing its inherent simplicity. My father always said what he meant and meant every word he said. The unpolished, sharp, hardened truth. If you asked for it, he would not disappoint. If you did not ask, chances are you would hear it anyway! Suffice it to say, my father's brand of honesty, while well intentioned for the most part, was not for everyone.

---

[12] Nelson Mandela, *Long Walk to Freedom* (New York: Little Brown & Co., 1994),

*NOTE: My father's name was spelled Aron on his birth certificate. Throughout his life he chose to spell his name Aaron in all legal, living records.

Granted, such candor was difficult to digest sometimes. One somber evening, as I stood alone in his room devastated by the aching realization his final hours were looming, emotions overwhelmed me. He responded with a voice that lacked the usual thunder yet still echoed with power, saying, "What the hell are you crying for? Everybody got to go when it's their time!" Imagine how jarring this proclamation was as I stood there, helpless and distraught wondering, "Will I even begin to repair the shattered pieces of my life without my father, the glue that helped keep it all together?" Regardless, I was all too familiar with my dad's logical approach to life by that time and while this grim declaration was not what I *wanted* to hear, I *needed* to acknowledge and eventually accept his sagacity. And today I am a far better man for it.

Stand briefly in my shoes and take in the moment as I did. I ask you to do this so you can understand a principle I swear by to this day; a fact that I believe will help those needlessly afraid of truth. In his darkest hour, my father reaffirmed that part of living an uncomplicated life meant viewing one's existence through the unobstructed lens of reality. Certain circumstances you can change, others you cannot. Plant your feet firmly on the ground, assess the situation, determine exactly how it affects you and modify it if you can. Do not question, do not vacillate, and do not second-guess. Act, accept and move on. This conviction, this dogged determination, this personal certitude is a form of freedom like no other. I believe that when you adopt this outlook you will find that you are no longer limited by fear, adversity, disappointment, or the need for validation.

By way of his original, prolific idioms and a life lived in accordance with his unconventional values, Aaron Lee Wallace, Jr. (aka Bigfoot) laid the foundation upon which I developed one of my favorite personal credos: When you completely accept who you are, you are in charge of your life! When you know who you are, what you stand for and that all your intentions are forthright, it will not matter what anyone labels you. To be able to sleep at night content in the knowledge you live righteously, guided by your Higher Power, is one of the most peaceful states of mind. You walk taller, you act with assurance, you speak with certainty, you carry yourself with dignity, you convey honesty and you embrace all this with humility.

Classify that attitude however you like. I know what it really is: giving honor to God by being a reflection of His goodness. Never be ashamed to wear that label proudly.

One thing I have discovered while writing this book is, what people say and to some degree how they say it can change a person's life. Especially the people we look up to and trust to guide us. I certainly take great care in the thoughts I convey on these pages because (my hope is) the words must help heal, support and encourage the reader to think in ways that will help them conquer their greatest obstacles. Words have tremendous power. They can stir the soul, lift spirits, and hurt deeply. It is important to speak responsibly. I explained that my dad's way of communicating could pack a bit of a sting. However, his words and his behavior, if considered carefully could have a palliative effect on lives overburdened by complex ways of thinking. Sometimes, a little tough love is necessary to shake us out of our insecurities and free us from our fears.

While my mother and father, the core of my beloved lineage, found great satisfaction in living a life unaffected by the thoughts, opinions and to a large extent the actions of others, they imparted their greatest lesson in the stoic way they lived life and accepted their own deaths. That acceptance proved to be the purest form of Freedom.

LEGACY

Your car's scheduled maintenance is a priority, but you can't visit your kids every day. You brag about how much you earn, and ignore your child, who you owe the most. Neglecting your kids is unacceptable! You hold their fragile life in your hands. Your deadbeat drama could make for an unhappy ending.

X

Urban legends can make for fascinating lore. Growing up in East Texas, I was always intrigued by the legends of Big Foot and the Loch Ness monster. I would read stories about their elusive sightings and wondered how these monstrous entities always managed to evade capture. And of course, what child did not settle into bed on Christmas Eve content in the certainty Santa Claus would find his way into their home (even without a chimney) and shower them with one whole year's worth of hopes and wishes; ample reward for their good behavior! Steeped in the innocence of youth, we invested fervent trust in this "man" we had never met personally and we would rest assured that this person would not disappoint us. Our callow hearts guaranteed that we walked by faith and not by sight. I fondly recall those sanguine years when young children were blissful and believed that all was right with the world.

There are days when I think about the present state of the family -especially with regard to fathers- and I fume at how much the men of my generation have notoriously espoused the fairytale existence I just described. They become absentee fathers and in some instances wear the moniker like a badge of honor. Few things are more ignoble than hearing a man gloat to anyone who will listen about how he avoids paying child support while gainfully employed, either by hiding the fact he earns a living or by lying about his income. I have personally overheard men boast shamelessly about evading their responsibilities and being unfazed by the demands, and most importantly the needs, of the family they helped create. They actually consider themselves resourceful. I call them reprehensible. These bold displays of hubris become even more egregious when they flaunt their blatant disregard for the children who become collateral damage in a battle of ego and thoughtlessness they were unwittingly born into. Mothers and family members are left to recount what has become a familiar tale, casually mentioning a "father" at family reunions or over Thanksgiving dinner. He is a man the children only hear about, a modern day urban legend. Some kids may have happened upon a faded picture of this "father", the image as cracked and distorted as the fractured relationship. Perhaps there was a chance sighting of a man with vaguely familiar eyes in the local mall or neighborhood supermarket. However hauntingly the tale unfolds, this man over time becomes as notorious and elusive as the mythical Big Foot. Unlike the fervent anticipation and hope that heralds the coming of St. Nick, this paternal apparition dredges up feelings of abandonment, loss and profound disappointment. As someone who understands and appreciates how critical foundation and structure are to laying the secure groundwork of a person's character, I find this missing link -the absent father- and its affect on a child's psyche disturbing.

Fortunately, as I have recounted so far, my familial experience was antithetic to this unpleasant scenario, much to my mental and emotional benefit. I cannot adequately impart how important it is to future generations to dispel the notion that being indifferent to your children is acceptable.

It is no secret how much my mother influenced my life. Alice Wallace touched all hearts in ways I can never fully articulate in this book or the others that may follow. Was her struggle unique? Not at all. Was she the first to overcome adversity or feel the sting of racism? Was she the first to challenge the status quo? Of course not. Did my mother change the world? Yes, she did. She changed *my* world. She altered *my* perception. She helped chart *my* course. However -and here is the key- she did not do it alone. Not by a long shot.

Ironically, I had a Bigfoot in my life. Note the difference in spelling. This larger than life entity was no fantasy or derelict dad. Aaron Lee Wallace, Jr., my father whose friends, colleagues, and family affectionately referred to as Bigfoot, was the genuine article. He personified commitment, sacrifice and stability. He was a pillar in the community and our Patriarch. My dad was a stern disciplinarian, loyal husband and dedicated father. He was quick-witted, sharp-tongued and had a heart that paralleled his hulking figure.

I was three years old when he met and courted my mother. A few months into their relationship, when she realized this man was destined to be a permanent part of our future, she revealed that she was battling a serious illness. This confession was a big step for a woman who rarely exposed her vulnerabilities. My father, undaunted, rejoined with a proposal and a wedding ring. As our family grew, he raised me as his oldest son. Moreover, I remain Aaron Wallace's son. Completely. Wholeheartedly. Woe to anyone who suggests differently today, or who suggested differently when he was alive. That is the kind of man my father was until the day he died. You may recall his final words to me before he passed on. "What the hell you crying for? Everybody got to go when it's their time!" He did not say this because he was mean-spirited or heartless. It was simply because he knew that his last act as a father had to be one of strength so that I could continue my journey courageously, knowing the man I loved, admired and respected expected nothing less. He led by example. If I am ever half the man he was, I will be a whole man. I looked up to him as a child does a hero.

Some of my dearest friends are women who, by an unfortunate twist of fate, must raise their children as single mothers. They are the strongest women I know yet their stories break my heart. A few of them were courageous enough to share their experiences, hoping the grief they imparted would in some way help change, and perhaps improve, how some men perceive fatherhood. Too many of these women admitted the men they were with intentionally chose to be an uninvolved parent for a myriad of selfish, inexcusable reasons. Some said that they were with men who felt -obviously too late- that they were not ready for children. Other men I am told did not love them, the mother of their child, enough to want to stick around. Then there were the men who had propagated so many children they could barely afford to take care of them. I was floored by these stories. It is as if these men were never taught the importance of being a father, a provider. Perhaps they did not have their own role models. Still, this is even more reason not to perpetuate the vicious cycle.

When couples part, one or both parties often sacrifice the children's well being. Child support stops, quality time ceases, one parent uses the kids as leverage to hurt the other. Children should not be victimized by drama. Dissolving a relationship does not absolve you from being responsible parents. For those who think that is acceptable, perhaps *you* are the one who needs to grow up.

This is a very difficult chapter to write. When you address such a delicate topic, and do so frankly, you run the risk of offending some people, which, of course, is not my intention. However, I will not mince words about how imperative it is to be an active, loving constant in the lives of your children and your family. I suspect those who are doing their best to be good fathers and providers will view these observations as affirmation that their efforts are not in vain, while those who have fallen short will undoubtedly take issue with the subject matter as it is presented here.

I view the role of fathers through the eyes of our family's beloved Bigfoot. I say, as he would, that most men can make moves, decisions, mistakes, plans, money, babies, love, war, progress and even make history. Not all men though, have what it takes to make a worthwhile difference in this world. Substance, drive, dedication, intelligence, faith and values all come from within. It is not what a man can make but what a man is made of that is impressive.

Not a single word that I have written should suggest that single moms are not equipped to lead a family. The foundation of any family is built upon love, discipline, history; attributes any dedicated, responsible parent, married or otherwise, can provide. However, I do believe that a family without a positive, supportive, loving male role model, who is available and perfectly capable of honoring his responsibility, is at a disadvantage. Yes, single mothers can do it. They have done it. Exceptionally well. My belief is they should not *have* to do it on their own. Men must stand up and be men. That means taking care of your children so they can have a worthwhile legacy.

During my conversations with women from various social, economic and professional backgrounds, I learned there was some confusion about what it means to need a man in their lives. I will not purport to tell anyone, especially women I do not know or whose experiences I cannot relate to, what she needs. I will reinforce the notion that it does not benefit anyone to choose independence simply because you want to *prove* you can do it alone. Alienating a man who is ready, willing and able to fulfill the important role of father is just as damaging to children and the sanctity of family as being a man who shuns the role. So much of who our children become is shaped by what they see; what they experience. Our young daughters watch their mothers and listen to what they say about their fathers or the men in their lives. Just for one moment ask yourself, am I being negative? Am I perpetuating disappointing expectations? On the other hand, am I teaching my daughter what she deserves in her relationship with men, especially her father who, after all is the first real substantial relationship she will have with a man? Men should ask themselves similar questions of their daughters and their sons. Am I setting a good example for a daughter who will one day be a girlfriend and a wife? For a son who will one day be a boyfriend and a husband? If we took more time to step outside of our ego and abandon resentment and bitterness in order to look pointedly and realistically at the lives we mold for our impressionable children, perhaps our decisions and actions would become more selfless. We would focus more on building our kids up, rather than breaking our mate down.

I never, ever saw my grandparents fight. Ever. I am sure my grandfather may have done any number of things to raise her ire. Granddad would always tell me, "Pick your battles big enough that they matter, but small enough that you can win." My grandmother's respect for him (actually their respect for each other) precluded any show of malice or flashes of anger. Now, my grandmother was no shrinking violet! She was the consummate matriarch and, I fear, part of a dying breed. Disagreements, I imagine, took place in private and never upset the daily workings of the household. Bear in mind, I acknowledged that my grandmother was a very strong woman despite the fact she never raised her voice or tried to prove her might in public displays of defiance. She carried herself in such a way that deference was paid by virtue of her standing in our family. Deference was paid because my grandfather never discredited her in our presence. Neither undermined the other. Instead, they understood each other in order to nurture their family.

Your children should have no greater role model than their parents and grandparents. If basketball players, rappers, actors and other non-parental influences are their primary guide they may end up lost. Your son or daughter should be a reflection of you. Hold a mirror up to your life. Is that an image they will be proud of? I hope it is, because that image could very well be their Legacy.

PHOENIX

Faith brings clarity. You stop asking why, and prepare for when. You accept that life's biggest disappointments can become the greatest blessings; when one door closes, another opens. When it does, step through fearlessly! If you walk in faith, you will not get lost.

XI

Like many of you, I have encountered difficulties in my life. I used to think, no one could possibly understand the extent of my pain. Nothing can even compare to the misery I feel. Well, through the years hard won lessons and an ample dose of maturity taught me that everyone's pain is relative. What may be a mild bump in the road to some could be a crippling landmine to others. It would serve us better to do away with observations like, "If it were me I would have . . .." Or, "If am ever faced with that situation I will . . ." Truth is we rarely know what we would, should, could or will do when facing a setback. Sure, given experiences and inherent knowledge of one's own behavior we can take an educated guess as to how we may react. However until one stands toe to toe with adversity only your Higher Power can say with any certainty whether you will stumble and fall, clear the hurdle, or both.

As I have shared with you, I lost my parents and my grandparents far too soon. I am not questioning the will of God. I am merely expressing my own selfish, but honest wish to have just one more day with each of them. Later in life, even as I still struggled to overcome my grief, I had to stand by as my children suffered life-altering crises that I could neither prevent nor make better. My marriage, despite my best efforts crumbled under the weight of irreconcilable differences precipitated by the fact we simply no longer wanted the same things. As we drifted apart, other aspects of my carefully laid out life fell to pieces.

It was about that time I was dismissed from a six-figure job. I had a family to support, a mortgage, car payments, and college tuition to pay. I needed a "Plan B". Failure was not an option. Therefore, I created a source of income that would keep us viable. I founded my company, Sol-Caritas. The revenue Sol generated helped us maintain the lifestyle we had become accustomed before I lost my job. I even improved our standard of living. No one ever knew I was out of work. Not my friends, my children or my siblings. Things were progressing well until another financial setback.

I lost tens of thousands dollars in an unsuccessful entertainment venture. Meanwhile, as I attempted to tally the fiscal damage, assess the fate of my marriage, mourn the loss of my lifelines, support my son's foray into a trying college football program and guide my daughter into the uncertainty of becoming a young woman, another disaster struck.

Exactly six days after saying good-bye to my dad, Hurricane Ike crippled Houston. Ike, at the time of this writing, was the costliest hurricane in Texas history. The storm wreaked havoc on my beloved city and the challenges and inconveniences that Ike left in its wake: deaths, widespread damage and impacts to the price and availability of oil and gas, only added to the mental, physical and spiritual burdens that had befallen me in a short span of time. I had come face to face with my biggest adversary: a life that seemed completely and perilously out of my control. I was in crisis.

To say that my faith and my courage were tested (and violently shaken) would be a gross understatement. Indulge me for a moment: stop and think about those moments in your own lives where you have literally been whipsawed by a constant, furious flow of misfortune. I am not a gambling man but I will wager that the last thing you were saying to yourselves was. "It's all good. Bring it on! What else do you have for me?" If you did, I tip my hat to you. I can assure you however, in my darkest hours, the light at the end of *my* tunnel was seriously obstructed because I was blinded by impaired faith.

One thing I refuse to do in life, and in this book, is present myself as some paradigm of strength impervious to suffering and heartache. We must own that aspect of our character that gives and bends through life's storms and pray that it does not snap. We also must not fear those moments where courage fails us because they are a reminder that we are human and remain a work in progress. At any time during those trying phases of my life, I could have given up. I could have found every excuse to surrender to my lot in life. I could have let my kids find their own way, given up my home, found another less fulfilling albeit practical means to subsist. However, I was not raised to concede. Quitting was not part of my make-up. My parents and grandparents were fearless and by the grace of God, I needed to be as well. The hardest decisions to make can sometimes be the most liberating. I was not about to let fear of short-term heartache interfere with my long-term happiness.

It was a slow, deliberate process, but I began to heal. I had to dig deep. Deeper than I ever had to. It was also an example of why I vehemently stress the importance of acknowledging and embracing your foundation. I reached back and drew upon memories that reawakened my spirit. I recalled that Granddaddy always reinforced the importance of being fiscally sound in order to stave off hardship. He would often reward me with two-dollar bills. It became our personal ritual. On special occasions, during our heart to heart talks, he would present me with the cherished currency and encourage me to save up for a rainy day. While I happily welcomed his generosity, it was not until much later in life that I appreciated the lesson attached. It was not the value of those two-dollar bills that pulled me out of my slump. Although I did have to tap those reserves in order to survive some days. It was the memory of a man and his grandson sharing a moment as rare as the gift he bestowed; a memory of what real love felt like. A love that said, "Baby -his term of endearment for me-, I have faith in you and I support you. I trust that you will always do the right thing in any circumstance using the means you are afforded. I believe you will not squander your opportunities or the resources you have at your disposal". During those talks, my grandfather was teaching me that no matter what the challenge, there would always be a way because I could make a way. I was actually doubly blessed because my Uncle Rube Earl shared the same wisdom and generosity each time he dropped a handful of coveted 50-cent pieces into my eager hands. His smile said, "You deserve this. You make me proud, and I know you will not be wanton with what others work hard to give you".

During those tortured moments, I still pondered how much I missed my momma. I would see her face and smell the scent of her love as if she was standing right beside me. I thought back to the days she would dress me in nice suits because she always wanted me to stand out and be taken seriously. Images of a precocious three year old dressed to impress and take on the world flooded my brain, washing away my insecurities and my apprehension. Despite all I was going through, I rediscovered my purpose. I stopped being afraid and realized I had much more to accomplish, a lot to prove, and a better life ahead.

When I surrendered to this rejuvenated mind, body and spirit, I was free to embrace the goodness that followed. I returned to work and reclaimed my unblemished record after a higher court determined the decision to terminate my position was unjustified. My marriage ended amicably and I met a woman who shared my vision, supported my goals and who was accomplished in her own right. A bond was formed that helped facilitate my next great accomplishment: I was hired to manage the *Top Dogs of Comedy*, one of the most renowned, sensational comedy groups. The remarkable success of the TDoC solidified my role as a leading player in the entertainment industry and ushered in a new era of growth and prosperity for Sol-Caritas and for me personally. As I chiseled away at the bonds that threatened to hold me back, I began to secure the ties that bind. I assembled staff, comics and executives who represent loyalty and commitment and friendship in every sense. It was no longer about my life, my company, my goals. Much like my treasured collection of two-dollar bills and 50-cent pieces, I was rewarded with a prized resource in the form of my valued team. These wonderful people transformed *me* into *us*. They became the soul of Sol.

Henry Ward Beecher wrote, "We should not judge people by their peak of excellence; but by the distance they have traveled from the point where they started."[13] I am grateful and fortunate to be able to say I have travelled a great distance. I want nothing more than to encourage you to do the same. In your darkest moments please remember that God has provided you with light. That light is your friends. That light is your circle of loved ones. That light is that voice within that reminds you no matter how badly you may feel now you will heal. You will overcome. Sometimes, the light comes from someone you least expect. Your light is within reach, sometimes just a phone call away. That's God making his presence known. Moreover, when you can, be the light someone else may need.

One of the biggest lessons I learned during my most trying periods is, never make decisions about your happiness, livelihood and long-term well-being based on anger, fear, loneliness, desperation, sadness or misguided expectations. When you are in any one of these states of being your resolve is weakened. Despair does not lend itself to clarity. Desperation diminishes

---

[13] Harriet Beecher Stowe, *Uncle Tom's Cabin* (Boston: The National Era Cleveland: John P. Jewett and Company, 1852),

your reason. Acting on either will only exacerbate an already dire situation. Be clear and focused before you commit to anything or anyone to avoid the pain of disappointment. It is so important to get a handle on your feelings and emotions, to get right with you in order to do what is right for you. Now, some people rise above challenges to overcome adversity. For others, overcoming adversity is an insurmountable challenge. Both attitudes are determined by your way of thinking.

Ultimately, you simply cannot dwell on your unhappiness or wallow in a vulnerable state. Ever. Instead, when you are faced with these human conditions ask yourself (seriously ask yourself) why am I here? Seek the answers that will help you free yourself from the shackles of discontent. Yes, we may not be "strong" all the time, but know this: we are all so much stronger than we give ourselves credit for. We just have to believe it.

Most clarity follows the darkest moments. That is just the way it is. Think about it; when was the last time you were feeling completely confident and everything was going as planned, and you thought to yourself euphorically, there is a lesson here? I understand"? I mean it's possible to have those "Aha" moments while basking in the glow of contentment but typically it happens after we've been knocked around a bit and we are emotionally, spiritually and physically exhausted by the very prospect of another minute of hopelessness. We stumble around, feeling our way through difficult issues, navigating complex relationships, gaining a better understanding of self through emotion and reason. The good thing is (well, it is more than good; it is critical to growth and enlightenment actually) every experience, interaction, conversation (even the negative ones) has a valuable lesson within. Sometimes the revelation is within reach. Other times we have to look deeper. Here is the key (and probably what scares a lot of us); we must be willing to see, hear, listen and accept what we learn about ourselves and about how we relate to others and life in general. When the lesson manifests itself make sure you *seriously and carefully* consider the message and make the necessary changes, so the difficult journey toward this answer was not in vain.

Sometimes, the hardest decisions we make are the most necessary. Walking away from a difficult situation is not always easy, especially if it is all you have ever known. However, you cannot let fear hold you hostage. You will not find peace if you surround yourself with the noise of dysfunction, misunderstanding, criticism and judgment from people around you. You will never be free if you are bound by insecurity, doubt and dependence. Weigh your options, plan carefully, prepare and pray. You may have to leave some people behind. If they end up in your rear view maybe they are not meant to be on this leg of the journey.

A Phoenix is defined as a mythical bird of great beauty fabled to live 500 or 600 years in the Arabian wilderness, to burn itself on a funeral pyre, and to rise from its ashes in the freshness of youth and live through another cycle of years: often an emblem of immortality or of reborn idealism or hope. When we shed the burdens that weigh us down you will discover, as I did, we all have what it takes to rise above our challenge. Inside all of us resides the heart of a Phoenix.

SUCCESS

Never apologize for the good in your life. People who try to make you feel badly because you have been blessed are consumed by self-loathing. Wear your accomplishments proudly, be it your career, your relationship, your children, your success. True friends will bask in the glow of your shine, not pray for darkness to fall.

XII

Success is constant. Any time you achieve more than you did the day before, the year before; any time you add a piece to the framework that will someday determine your ultimate goal, you have achieved some degree of success. My encounters with some very inspiring individuals revealed that the success so many of us crave will be appreciated after death. I can recall several great historical icons whose contribution to their respective fields, in my opinion, became evident as a nation mourned. Dr. Martin Luther King. Jr, Mother Theresa, Franklin Delano Roosevelt, John Fitzgerald Kennedy and Jesus Christ, to name a few.

Then there are those legends of pop culture that society raised to levels of excellence: Michael Jackson, Whitney Houston, Marvin Gaye, TuPac Shakur and John Lennon, all artists whose contribution to the music industry appeared to resonate more profoundly in various forms of requiem. And of course, how can I not mention cultural icons such as Picasso, Mozart and Shakespeare, whose works grew in value exponentially after they had been laid to rest.

I would like to share my personal experience with how this revelation manifested. Growing up in a tight knit community, it was common to find one or two people who clearly stood apart as a leader. Someone we could turn to in times of grief, challenge, and despair. In Jacksonville, that person was Stacy, a friend to all who knew him.

Stacy was larger than life. Not only in stature but also in character. He led by example and set the bar high. You would be hard-pressed to find a kinder, smarter, stronger and more compassionate man. He was every mother's favorite son, every man's hero and every pastor's example of Christian spirit. Stacy never backed down from a fight but he never went looking for one either. He was always there to protect someone from, and to mediate skirmishes. Young men viewed him as a mentor. Young women, the kind of man they would marry or have their daughters date. His life was dedicated to the service of others; a selfless, sincere individual who left an indelible mark on the lives of everyone he touched. And he touched thousands of lives. Take my word for it. I do not exaggerate the measure of his influence. At his funeral there was not enough room in the church to accommodate the sheer multitude of mourners who gathered to pay homage to an individual every single person in attendance admitted, changed their life. There were men and women, teenagers and young children present to testify about of this hometown hero. His generous deeds outnumbered the loved ones who hugged, cried and remembered his amazing legacy. Stories of kind acts (some we never even knew about) weaved throughout the pews and the congregation. I could not help but think to myself, *this* is the true evidence of success. No amount of money, property or businesses could outweigh the hope and inspiration and the happy and healed hearts that Stacy left behind. I am not certain if he ever knew how many lives he transformed. However, what *is* important is that he did. The ones he guided will carry his mission forward and (I pray) continue his purposeful acts now that he has gone to glory. I know now that one must live as we wish to be remembered.

My grandfather exemplified that credo. A man of distinction and principles, his journey to success was hard won. It also laid the groundwork I follow. From his days working on the railroad to his ascent to prominent Justice, he remained steadfast. And he accomplished all this while raising a family with a woman, my beloved grandmother, whom he was married to until death. My grandmother would share stories about their good times and bad moments and never once did she so much as hint about a time they considered separating. Respect played a great role in their union. They both appreciated the other's value in their lives. Whatever their issues, neither, it seemed, ever felt they were anything less than an important part of the whole. First Corinthians 13: 4-8 reads: "Love is patient, love is kind. It does not envy, it does not boast, it is not proud. It does not dishonor others, it is not self-seeking, it is not easily angered, it keeps no record of wrongs. Love does not delight in evil but rejoices with the truth. It always protects, always trusts, always hopes, always perseveres. Love never fails. But where there are prophecies, they will cease; where there are tongues, they will be stilled; where there is knowledge, it will pass away." My grandparents' lived these words. I consider their marriage (their long-standing relationship) the highest level of success.

Please remember, this is all a process. As you chase success, and probably abuse your own feelings and mental stability to get it, make sure you have a clear understanding of this sometimes elusive goal. If you judge that label based solely on other people's accomplishments, financial gain and material possessions, know this: bank accounts may overflow, but what good is wealth if one is spiritually, emotionally, and mentally bankrupt. This is part of the reason people feel so dejected at times. Why being strong is so difficult. We see what we *think* we want, and what we *think* will make us happy. We are not fulfilled. We force ourselves to put on this armor against life in order to arrive at this set destination, armor intended to "protect" us from the day to day arsenal of negative forces; yet we have done very little to reinforce the heart and soul and even less to build and heal our minds.

Nothing substantive in our lives can be achieved if we lack the mental, physical and spiritual wherewithal to determine what we want and comprehend what to do with it once we get it. This is all personal. It has absolutely nothing to do with how someone else climbed the ladder of success. The more you focus on that, the greater the likelihood you will miss a critical rung on your ascent. You need to get right, before you can be all right.

Obviously, when fighting our battles we all hope to be soldiers. Sometimes though, our experiences can take a burdensome toll. Whether we are clashing with life, with others or with ourselves, there may come a time we just want to give up. We get tired. We get discouraged. We become casualties in the fight. Moreover, we wonder why every time we take one step forward, circumstances knock us back three steps. Then, we look around and see "everybody else doing so well"; we notice everyone achieving his or her goals, becoming successful. It is as if they do not have a care in the world. Well, therein lays an extremely self-destructive perception.

Take a step back and be reasonable. Realistically, you cannot possibly know how everybody is doing. There are far too many people in the world for that to be even remotely possible. Let's keep it in perspective. Secondly, you have no idea what the people around you, or whom you see on t-v, in movies, magazines, etc., had to sacrifice in order to realize their personal *success*. Sometimes, greatness -whatever that may be-comes at a substantial cost. Be careful what you hope for, you just might get it. Sometimes the "it" that comes with the success you want so badly is divorce, depression, money problems, betrayal by friends and family, loss of privacy, health issues. All that glitters isn't gold.

No one can tell you how long you will be on the path to finding inner peace and self-acceptance. Lord knows I can't. I have pitched many a tent along the road myself as I seek the spot to build a permanent spiritual domicile. Nevertheless, I know I must do the work. I need to do the work because one thing is for sure; I will never be satisfied until those days where I feel "something is missing" are less frequent and eventually extinct! So, by all means, chase your dreams! But understand, you have to be prepared on all fronts if you expect to enjoy your life!

And please, be precise in your ambition. If you set your sights in too many directions, you cannot focus. If you do not designate a concrete, attainable goal, than there is no usable conduit to success. You're stuck. If you have a goal and do not work at it, night and day, against all odds; if you are not dedicated, excited, encouraged and willing to fight for it, you are stuck. If you are basing your effort, your progress and your accomplishments on your peers, you are stuck. And I do not mean adding a healthy dose of competitiveness to your daily cocktail of motivation. I mean literally looking to your left and to your right and saying, "I will never be that good no matter how hard I try". By putting that negative death knell out into the Universe you have doomed yourself to being stuck. Norman Vincent Peale wrote, "Believe in yourself! Have faith in your abilities! Without a humble but reasonable confidence in your own powers you cannot be successful or happy."[14]

I cringe each time I hear anyone blame another person, group of persons, an organization or any external force for their shortcomings. How can it be that you, an adult, cannot succeed in life because someone or something will not let you? Whether it is your boss, a family member or someone you are in a relationship with, no

---

[14]   Norman Vincent Peale, *The Power of Positive Thinking* (New York: Fawcett Crest, 1952)

one can prevent you from accomplishing great things but you. The same power you give to people that you claim hold you back, use to knock them out of your way. Rationalization is effective when solving legitimate problems. However, some people have raised it to some delusionary art form and use it to mask poor judgment or excuse their lack of motivation. Do not be blinded by this misconception. Bad decisions with good intentions are *still* bad decisions. Sitting idly by, letting life and opportunity pass you by because you are being held down by circumstances only leaves you stuck in a rut and hating the world for a condition you created. Sugarcoat your reasons all you like; the outcome will still leave a sour taste. It may be a difficult reality to grasp but sometimes, the only person who is in your way is you.

There comes a time, in everyone's life, where you must stop caring what everyone else thinks, what someone else is saying, and how other people feel about how you choose to live or you will go insane. We cannot call ourselves adults or masters of our own destiny if we are always looking for people to co-sign our every move. It is hard enough meeting your own expectations sometimes. Why add the burden of trying to reach those of people who probably do not even have their own acts together? Just be who you are. Kindhearted, harsh, no nonsense, flaky, arrogant, wild, subdued, adventurous, spiritual, atheistic, high maintenance, easygoing, successful, still struggling. Whatever the case, just be that person. Do not make excuses. Do not try to transform into a person someone wants you to become. And, if one day you want to make some changes, do it for yourself. Adjust to your own taste.

Ultimately, you cannot expect to steer your own life, if you keep handing over the keys. I explained in the last chapter, how fortunate I am to have assembled a top-notch team of staff and executives at Sol-Caritas. Once you embark on the road to success, keep in mind: the company you keep determines how others view you. Identify with mediocrity and you will be labeled sub par. Collaborate with questionable people and your own reputation becomes suspect. Guilt by association can end a career, hurt your business and cost you friends. How unfortunate, to be condemned for someone else's sins? Choose your alliances wisely. If you are not comfortable introducing a person to your friends and family or you hesitate to bring them around colleagues or business partners, chances are (actually it is pretty much a sure thing) they will do more to cramp your style than help your image. Align yourself with people who will uplift, support encourage and reflect who you really are. Do not let poor judgment keep you from a life you richly deserve.

I have often been asked, "How do you remain so focused?" and I think to myself, the real question should not be how, but why. Pubilius Syrus wrote, "To do two things at once, is to do neither well".[15] This is a key message. The brain can only focus on one specific action at a time. You can have a million things on your mind (and many of us do). However, I think most people can effectively analyze, process and be completely attentive to one thought. Therefore, cluttering your brain with nonsense like the negative musings of people who do not contribute a single thing to your well-being means you are taking your focus away from things that matter. Trying to multi-task means, you are taking your focus off each important action you are trying to complete. Yes, we all must juggle family, career and hobbies as we force ourselves to have these full lives. That is fine, but understand you run the risk of neglecting one for the other because *you cannot give 100% to more than one thing!* So stop beating yourself up about it. Stop trying to counteract one of your body's complex physiological realities!

---

[15]   Publius Syrus, *The Moral Sayings of Publius Syrus: A Roman Slave (1855)* (Whitefish: Kessinger Publishing, 2008)

Instead of trying to keep pace, just pace yourself! Sometimes you need to do a hundred things. I get it. But ask yourself, what happens when you do that? You burn out! And the next hundred things you need to do, suffer. Keep it in perspective. Set limits, set goals, establish "to-do" lists in order of priority. More importantly though, practice focus. Get your mind right. One day at a time, one task at a time, one life to live. Each deserves your undivided attention.

Today, seek your own approval. Encourage yourself. Do something that benefits you and your future. And above all, be proud of your accomplishments, no matter who else acknowledges them! You should always be your greatest motivator. Never leave that power in someone else's hands. Once you learn to love the person you are, there are no limits to the person you can become; there are no limits to your Success.

HUNT

ONEAL
JUNE 27, 1914
JULY 17, 1998

ELNORA G.
NOV 6, 1918
AUG. 12, 2000

JUSTICE OF THE PEACE 1983 - 1996 PRECINCT 2 ANDERSON CO.

142

FORWARD

Windshields are bigger than rear view mirrors for a reason, life is meant to live forward rather than the opposite. With any living creature on this planet we call earth; growth is a constant evolution and natural state. No one or nothing with life is meant to remain the same as its beginning, but to experience the phases of what develops it to be whole. The layers of life in which we compile thru life experiences are the product of who we are at that moment in time.

XIII

The day I began this final chapter I was overcome with a flood of emotions. I knew that writing a book would not be easy. It was not a literary exercise I pursued casually. After all, these words will one day speak for me when I am unable to speak for myself. Therefore, the message had to be thoughtful, uncompromising, detailed and above all profoundly meaningful. I was *not* prepared however, for how much this deeply personal labor of love would transform me.

One morning, I laid all the pages out on my desk and soaked up every word, every chapter. My senses came alive! I methodically scanned the document line by line and watched my life over the years leap poignantly off the once blank, stark white sheets; canvases upon which I illustrated the who, what, where and why of my humble existence. I solemnly revisited my past through tears and smiles. I could hear the whispered voices of my nearest and dearest telling me that the practical wisdom they imparted must be shared. The experiences that helped mold me must be shared. The pain and redemption must be shared, because someone somewhere is lost and alone and I, by virtue of my own trials and triumphs, may hold the key that unlocks their salvation.

As I added the finishing touches to my first book, it suddenly dawned on me: an effort intended to help the reader find order in the midst of chaos and simplicity buried under the weight of complications, became my cathartic journey of self-discovery.

A recurring theme throughout this book has been that we often take our past for granted. We regard our upbringing, relationships and family ties with cursory interest, tucking moments and encounters away as we would a favorite blanket or souvenir that has outlived its usefulness and relevance. Yet as I recovered memories, explored experiences and carefully examined the lessons that inspired the man I am today, I discovered that in order for anyone to move forward we must know and understand our past. The key is to *learn* from our history, not to dwell there. We must not become entangled in the emotional cobwebs and shadows that linger ominously in the recesses of our intellect. Nor should we ignore the bygone days altogether. Instead, we must make a conscience decision to audit our yesterdays in order to build worthwhile tomorrows.

People who know me are familiar with my penchant for metaphors. I find it easier to explain complex points-of-view by painting relatable pictures for the listener. In order to illustrate my take on life, I have likened it to travelling on a long, winding stretch of road. We drive along meandering paths, dodging potholes, hugging treacherous curves. We also (hopefully) take in the beauty of the changing landscapes ahead of us and on the periphery. We do all this with our eyes forward as the scene ahead comes at us full speed through the windshield. Meantime, we steal glances at the rear view mirror catching glimpses of the places we have been; images that become smaller as the distance increases. The vast expanse of the windshield in comparison to the rear-view is clearly by design. The opposing dimensions say it all. After all, when you are moving forward it is more important to see where you are headed versus where you have been. Well I believe this concept parallels life. Every living creature on earth evolves and grows; moves forward. Nothing stays the same. We all change. That is just a basic fact of life. You can resist but you cannot prevent the manifestation of this constant. Unless you plan to remain virtually dormant socially, mentally, emotionally and physically -which contradicts the natural physiology of healthy living creatures- the path before you must be vast and unobstructed and essentially, your primary focus

The road to personal enlightenment can be long and drawn out. To put it in some perspective, the content in this book has taken me *42 years* to compile. I attempted to start the project a few times in the last 3 years, but the timing never seemed quite right. The story as you now know began rather dramatically on the hardwood during a contentious basketball game. My mother eventually defeated her toughest competition that night despite the obstacles, known and unknown, before her! That experience has forever served as the prelude to my life and now, of this book. That said, it became apparent that while my experiences were invaluable to *me*, this book had to appeal to and benefit a larger audience; serve a greater purpose if you will. Poet John Donne put it best: "No man is an island, entire of itself; every man is a piece of the continent a part of the main".[16] We all have something to offer one another. I needed to produce a timeless resource that friends, family and perfect strangers alike could turn to for encouragement.

I do not have all the answers. What I do have is a burning desire to honor the memory of my parents and grandparents and my beloved uncle

---

[16] John Donne, "John Donne, "Devotions upon emergent occasions and Seuerall steps in my Sickness - Meditation XVII, 1624,"," (London: Printed by A. M. for Thomas Jones, 1624).

Rube Earl. To be the kind of person who shares blessings. Moreover, at the risk of stating the obvious, the simplest things in our lives help us achieve the greatest blessings. Thankfully, none of those things cost a thing. Yet they reap abundant rewards. Faith, honesty and good manners will take you to the far reaches of success and help secure rewards money never will. I hope this book will be one of your blessings.

The pages herein are replete with experiences that are relatable to just about everyone. More importantly, many of us, including those who read the book share a common feeling: knowing we are not alone in our struggles. And we all struggle to some degree. Some in big ways, others small, but as the adage goes, "Into each life some rain must fall". A poor man's struggle may be finding his next meal. A rich man's challenge is finding (and keeping) the trust of his inner circle. The extent of their trials is relative of course. Yet this should not detract from the fact that they are each troubled.

I am not foolish enough to think this book is a cure for what ails the general populous, but I hope it at least offers some direction. Often times we know the answer we are seeking and we simply need some guidance. When I was about 23, I was devastated by a series of traumatic events that unfolded during a short period. My employer suggested it might be a good idea to seek the advice of a professional therapist. During the session, I laid my heartache bare for about 30 minutes. Before the one-hour appointment even ended, the therapist looked at me and said "Mr. Wallace your only problem is you need someone to talk to." Those words are imprinted indelibly on my brain and I always try to follow her advice. Admittedly, there were times when I could not find the words or the right ear to bend. That said, I pray that the words I have shared are healing for the reader.

I have discovered that life is about establishing a foundation, finding purpose, overcoming adversity, respecting your legacy, being fearless, rising above disappointment while striving toward success. Do your best to navigate your respective paths, stay the course and always focus on moving forward. Focus on peace of mind. I look around at the time and expense so many people make to improve their physical appearance. We go to great lengths to shed physical weight. That is not much good if your mental health is loaded down. Dishonest, selfish, miserable people are poison. If they are in your life, your social circle needs a detox. Nothing reduces useless negativity like dropping dead weight.

Ultimately, the goal of this book is to help simplify the way we think about things; simplify the way we react to the words or actions of other people. Your life is not so complicated. God has already written the script, casted the key players. It is when we try to re-write the plot that we encounter unnecessary drama. Accept the role God has chosen you to play. Faith in his direction will assure an Oscar worthy performance!

I wish my loved ones could have lived to see this day. My mom would have been so very proud! As a matter of a fact if she was still with us she would have purchased and personally sold enough copies of this book to propel it to number one on the *"New York Times Best Seller"* list. My mom was by far my biggest cheerleader.

My dad would have been a bit more composed, and rather reserved with his praise. He would want to be assured I did not offend anyone. Granddaddy would insist that I maintained a strict level of dignity, honesty and professionalism. His mantra: "If you are going to do it, do it right. If you do not have all of the tools needed to execute it properly, wait until you do. Above all, never question God's timing. He knows best". And Mubba, ever cautious, would urge me to remain vigilant because the devil is always working. She would also remind me to keep smiling saying "You look more inviting".

These principles, these people, shaped my life. I have been blessed with the guidance of the ages, the patience of my loved ones and the grace of God. It gives me pleasure to offer all that I have learned to you. Please, take what you need.

I will leave you with this: Each day, speak as if someone may be listening in and act as if someone could be watching. Do not say it if you do not mean it or know it to be true. Do not do anything privately that would shame you publicly. Good judgment should not cease simply because you think no one will ever know. Everything performed in the darkness is always revealed in the light. The Universe has an uncanny way of laying your life bare. Make sure you can deal with what may eventually be revealed. It is as simple as that.

In the end, you control your own destiny. Life does not have to be so complicated. When in doubt, let go, and let God. If you say this, mean it. If you believe it, then practice what you preach. Words, and faith, will only take you as far as your actions allow. Do your best to ensure those actions always lead you Forward.

FLOWERS

The loss of loved ones always saddens me. Not only because they are no longer with us. But because it reminds me how much we take each other for granted. We just presume they will be there. We trust that there will be time to let them know they are loved and appreciated. And their passing, especially if it is unexpected fills us with grief and sometimes regret.

The people in my life that mattered the most died far too soon. Nothing hurts more than knowing that my parents and grandparents did not live to see how much they influenced every aspect of my life. I am not able to thank them for everything they taught me. I will never know if I am truly meeting their expectations despite my best efforts.

While I mourned my dearly departed I cherished family that was still living. My uncle Rube Earl was my by far a treasured favorite in that category. He was the one I shared my accomplishments with, the one I would call when I was worried or confused. Moreover Uncle Rube was the only relative I could not wait to present with a copy of this book. I kept it a secret. I wanted to surprise him. I pictured the expression on his face, which had become drawn and weary, a consequence of his long battle with cancer. He would grin, and his features would brighten as he read how he, Mom, Dad, Granddaddy and Mubba inspired me. Soft spoken and strong-willed, he would urge me to persevere and never rest laurels. All while beaming with pride! His gentle laugh would wash over me, comfort me, remind me that my roots are anchored deep. A discreet reassurance that he would always be a source of support.

I replayed this scenario so many times. Sadly, I would never be able to experience that moment with my Uncle Rube. He succumbed to cancer on July 19, 2013. Up until that day he was the only living kin mentioned in this book. Regretfully, I had let an opportunity to share that fact with him, slip away. However well intentioned my motives were, there will forever be a void in my heart. This reality check rekindled a truth I have always known but often disregarded. Life is too short to wait until "tomorrow".

Many of us lead busy lives. We juggle careers, family and extracurricular activities while trying to pay bills, set up nest eggs, chase our dreams, raise children, perhaps care for aging parents all as we struggle to maintain our sanity in the process. Throw in a desire to exercise and (for many) meditate, worship and sleep and you can use up every second of your day. Thing is, while we are doing all we can to survive the day-to-day grind and live up to our responsibilities, we neglect a basic human need: The need for affection. The need to love and be loved.

Establishing a connection, a bond, is essential to sustaining positive meaningful relationships with the people you are working so hard to support and who support you. The people who we want to make proud. One should never be too busy to take a moment to express a thought or loving word or share good news. These are the moments that link hearts. They are the ties that bind.

Never lose sight of the people who are the foundation of the future you are working to build. Foster and reinforce that element of your life and you will surely strengthen your destiny.

Love is meant to be expressed. Love shouldn't be bound by rules or conditions. Hidden or doled out in small doses. You must not give "just enough". Suppressing the kindness stifles its effects and extinguishes its fire, robbing the special people in your life of a healing gift. You gain so much from its free, wholehearted expression. When given from the heart love benefits the giver and the receiver.

It will be difficult for me to heal from the loss of my beloved Uncle. He was an exceptional mentor and one of my most ardent supporters and trusted confidants. What will hurt the most, and for some time though, is knowing there was so much left unsaid. We speak so dearly of the dead at funerals and at the first dinner or reunion following their death. And often we wonder, "Did they know how much they were love and appreciated?". That question may haunt me for some time to come. Please do all you can to avoid this feeling of regret. Show love today. Show love tomorrow. Show love often. Show love always.

The late Joan Crawford once famously said, ""*Send me flowers while I'm alive. They won't do me a damn bit of good after I'm dead.*" Truer words were never spoken.

IN REMEMBRANCE OF OUR BELOVED

ENTERED
LIFE
June 11,
1949

ENTERED
ETERNITY
July 19,
2013

Mr. Rube Earl Hicks

ACKNOWLEDGMENTS

First and foremost I would like to thank my Lord and Savior for blessing me with more than I could ever deserve. For giving me the knowledge, no-how and patience to complete this mission, I am forever grateful.

I would also like to acknowledge Dr. John Nadalin, thank you for helping me see beyond my vision and touch lives I never knew I could reach. To Liz Faublas at Million $ Pen, Ink. for not allowing me to settle for simplicity and for helping put the best of my life in words for personal perfection.

Special thanks to my wonderful staff at Sol-Caritas / Alice Wallace Foundation; Kimberly Vopat, Missy Franklin, Wendy Alford, Bernadette Jenkins and Chrystal Rivers for the daily dedication and commitment to helping me help others.

My dedication to charity guides my purpose. The love of laughter inspires my vision. The generous support of supporters, friends and fans along with the finest businesses in Houston and throughout America helps drive my mission. Thank you to those who generously donate to one or all of the charities Sol-Caritas supports.

Honorable Discharge

from the Armed Forces of the United States of America

This is to certify that

RM3 CARLOS (NMN) WALLACE, USN, █████████

was Honorably Discharged from the

United States Navy

on the ___2ND___ day of ___MARCH 1992___ *This certificate is awarded*

as a testimonial of Honest and Faithful Service

C. M. DURHAM, GS-7

SEPARATION BRANCH SUPERVISOR

58N (REV. 6-50)

The Giving Back Group

To all to whom these presents shall come, Greeting

Be it known that

Carlos Wallace

having honorably fulfilled all the requirements imposed by the authorities of this Institution, the President and the trustees of The Giving Back Group, upon recommendation of the faculty, do therefore confer the degree of

Altruism

with all the Honors, Rights, and Privileges to that degree appertaining.

Roger Contreras

University President

Ginger Contreras

Vice President

HelpingaHero.org

September 12, 2012

Carlos Wallace
2115 Medway Dr
The Woodlands, TX 77386

Dear Carlos Wallace,

Thank you for your generous donation to support HelpingaHero.org's effort to build adapted homes for our wounded veterans who have sacrificed so much for our freedom. With your help, HelpingaHero.org has achieved new heights of success this year. We have awarded 30 homes in the last 12 months and will award another 20+ homes at our annual Gala on October 24, 2012. This national event will be held in Houston and will honor former Commander-in-Chief, President George W. Bush, who will receive the Patriot Award. Comedian Dennis Miller will serve as the Master of Ceremonies.

We are also pleased to announce that one of our heroes has been selected for the final episode of *Extreme Makeover: Home Edition* which will air in December 2012, on your local ABC station. Be sure to tune in for this 2-hour holiday edition featuring Staff Sergeant Shilo Harris, U.S. Army (Ret.) and HelpingaHero.org.

Your continued financial support will enable us to continue helping our veterans rebuild their lives with the security of a new home that has been fully adapted to their physical needs. For a list of upcoming ground breakings and home presentations, visit our website www.helpingahero.org. We hope you will be able to attend one of our upcoming home presentations and share in the joy as we officially present a set of house keys to one of our wounded heroes.

Sincerely,

Chris Dewhurst
Chairman of the Board
HelpingaHero.org

HelpingaHero.org Federal Tax ID is 20-5433598

5910 Rose Street, Houston, TX 77007
Toll Free: 888-786-9531 Fax: 281-246-4324
www.helpingahero.org donate@helpingahero.org

SHOOT2SCORE™

Sol-Caritas

C/O Carlos Wallace

PO Box 531

Spring, TX 77383

To Carlos Wallace and the Sol-Caritas team:

I would like to thank you very much for what your monthly comedy show at the Improv brings to the community of Houston, Texas. Laughs are a great way for people to come together as one, and you all have found a way to package that into a great show as well as a chance to highlight local charities that give back in our community.

Shoot 2 Score Hoops is very grateful for the donation and the chance to speak to the audience about how we teach young kids the game of life on and off the basketball court.

Again, my company and the kids we serve definitely appreciate you guys for what you do. I hope that we can partner on more events in the future.

In the Movement,

Marcus Sloan

Shoot 2 Score Hoops, CEO

www.shoot2scorehoops.com

SOL-CARES
2012
PROUDLY SUPPORTED:

Covenant House
Thomas Routt Foundation
Impact Center
SHS Volleyball Booster Club
Lexington Woods Swim Team
Generation Gap Youth Sports
SAYS — Spring Softball
Top Ladies of Distinction, Inc
Top Teens of America
Houston Area Women's Center
Lupus Foundations of America
American Diabetes Association
American Cancer Society
Yele Haiti Organization
Treyvon Martin Memorial Foundation
Saint Tower Academy
Organization of Black Aerospace Professionals
Helping A Hero
Dynamic Kids
Shoot 2 Score
Houston Pink Book
Help, Hope & Love
Tri-Country Youth Football
Ana's Angels
Modify
Keey 2 Kids
Pancho Claus
Shoebox Recycling
Tamina Community Center

www.sol-caritas.com